THIS BOOK GIVEN TO

_____

GIVEN BY

_____

DATE

_____

What if your Blessings come through raindrops?

Freeman-Smith, a division of Worthy Media, Inc.

134 Franklin Road, Suite 200, Brentwood, Tennessee 37027

The quoted ideas expressed in this book (but not Scripture verses) are not, in all cases, exact quotations, as some have been edited for clarity and brevity. In all cases, the author has attempted to maintain the speaker's original intent. In some cases, quoted material for this book was obtained from secondary sources, primarily print media. While every effort was made to ensure the accuracy of these sources, the accuracy cannot be guaranteed. For additions, deletions, corrections, or clarifications in future editions of this text, please write Freeman-Smith.

"Blessings" © 2011 New Spring Publishing (ASCAP) / Laura Stories (ASCAP). All rights for the world on behalf of Laura Stories administered by New Spring Publishing. All Rights Reserved. Used By Permission.

Scripture quotations are taken from:

The Holy Bible, King James Version (KJV)

The Holy Bible, New International Version (NIV) Copyright © 1973, 1978, 1984, by International Bible Society. Used by permission of Zondervan Publishing House. All rights reserved.

The Holy Bible, New King James Version (NKJV) Copyright © 1982 by Thomas Nelson, Inc. Used by permission.

Holy Bible, New Living Translation, (NLT) copyright © 1996. Used by permission of Tyndale House Publishers, Inc., Wheaton, Illinois 60189. All rights reserved.

The Message (MSG)- This edition issued by contractual arrangement with NavPress, a division of The Navigators, U.S.A. Originally published by NavPress in English as THE MESSAGE: The Bible in Contemporary Language copyright 2002-2003 by Eugene Peterson. All rights reserved.

New Century Version®. (NCV) Copyright © 1987, 1988, 1991 by Word Publishing, a division of Thomas Nelson, Inc. All rights reserved. Used by permission.

International Children's Bible®, New Century Version®. (ICB) Copyright © 1986, 1988, 1999 by Tommy Nelson™, a division of Thomas Nelson, Inc. All rights reserved. Used by permission.

The New American Standard Bible®, (NASB) Copyright © 1960, 1962, 1963, 1968, 1971, 1972, 1973, 1975, 1977, 1995 by The Lockman Foundation. Used by permission.

The Holman Christian Standard Bible™ (HCSB) Copyright © 1999, 2000, 2001 by Holman Bible Publishers. Used by permission.

Cover Design by Daniel McCarthy / Concept Culture
Page Layout by Bart Dawson

ISBN 978-1-60587-322-0

WHAT IF YOUR

BLESSINGS

COME THROUGH RAINDROPS?

LAURA STORY

A DEVOTIONAL BASED ON THE GRAMMY AWARD WINNING
#1 SONG THAT HAS INSPIRED MILLIONS

Table of Contents

Anyone who meets a testing challenge
head-on and manages to stick it out
is mighty fortunate.
For such persons loyally in love
with God, the reward
is life and more life.

—

James 1:12 MSG

Lyrics from the Grammy-nominated song

"BLESSINGS"

BY LAURA STORY

We pray for blessings,
We pray for peace
Comfort for family, protection while we sleep
We pray for healing, for prosperity
We pray for Your mighty hand to ease our suffering
And all the while, You hear each spoken need
Yet love us way too much to give us lesser things

'Cause what if Your blessings come through raindrops?
What if Your healing comes through tears?
What if a thousand sleepless nights are what it takes
to know You're near?
What if trials of this life are Your mercies in disguise?

We pray for wisdom,
Your voice to hear
We cry in anger when we cannot feel You near
We doubt your goodness, we doubt Your love
As if each promise from Your Word is not enough
And all the while, You hear each desperate plea
And long that we'd have faith to believe

’Cause what if Your blessings come through raindrops?
What if Your healing comes through tears?
What if a thousand sleepless nights are what it takes
to know You’re near?
What if trials of this life are Your mercies in disguise?

When friends betray us
When darkness seems to win,
We know that pain reminds this heart,
That this is not our home

’Cause what if Your blessings come through raindrops?
What if Your healing comes through tears?
What if a thousand sleepless nights are what it takes
to know You’re near?
What if trials of this life are Your mercies in disguise?

What if my greatest disappointments,
Or aching of this life,
Is the revealing of a greater thirst this world
can’t satisfy.
What if trials of this life,
The rain, the storms, the hardest nights
Are Your mercies in disguise?

ABOUT "BLESSINGS"

❦

The song "Blessings" is about just that: the redefining of blessings in my own life. As a child, I grew up hearing songs like "God Bless America" and saying "the blessing" every time we ate a meal. Although patriotic songs and mealtime prayers are wonderful, they may have conveyed a subtle message that was decidedly unhelpful—they taught me that God's blessings always arrive in the form of health, happiness, and prosperity.

But, where does that leave the other things that come into our lives? If I experience hardship or heartbreak, am I being punished? If my husband has poor health, is that a curse from God? Some may think so.

When my husband Martin was first diagnosed with a brain tumor, well-meaning strangers asked him if he had any unconfessed sin in his life, for surely God would not curse him for no reason. But the more my husband and I looked to God's Word, the more we came to realize that sometimes God actually blesses His children through the absence of the very things they pray for.

Paul asked God to remove the thorn from His flesh; instead, God chose to teach Paul about a power that is only made perfect in weakness. Job deeply mourned the loss of his possessions and his health, yet he learned to worship God in the midst of his nakedness.

So how do I define blessings now? I'm still not sure. Every "what if" of the song "Blessings" symbolizes a thousand questions God seems to have left unanswered. But this I do know: There is a depth of intimacy with God that can only be known through suffering. There is a reliance on Him that can only be experienced when everything else around my soul seems to give way. And if that's what it takes to make this stubborn child cling to that old rugged cross, you can have your prosperity.

I'd rather have Jesus.

CHAPTER 1

BLESSED TO BE A BLESSING

Now the LORD had said to Abram:
"Get out of your country, from your family and from
your father's house, to a land that I will show you.
I will make you a great nation; I will bless you and
make your name great; and you shall be a blessing."

—

Genesis 12:1-2 NKJV

In order to understand what God's blessings are, we must answer an important question: Why does God bless His children? Does God simply operate a straightforward reward system for good behavior? Or does He have other plans and purposes?

The story of Abraham has much to teach us about God's blessings. In Genesis 12, we learn how God made a promise to Abraham, a promise to bless him with countless descendants. And when He fulfilled His promise, God not only answered Abraham and Sara's longing to have children, but He also created the nation of Israel.

> In the very place where God has put us, whatever its limitations, whatever kind of work it may be, we may indeed serve the Lord Christ.
> —*Elisabeth Elliot*

We have no reason to believe that Abraham had done anything to merit God's good favor. In fact, as we read on, we discover that Abraham's behavior was far from perfect; Abraham's life had been tarnished by lying and manipulation, stemming from his root sin of unbelief. Yet, God kept His promise.

So, what was God's reason for blessing Abraham? God blessed him "to be a blessing." God's blessing upon Abraham was given for a specific purpose: so that Abraham might, in turn, be a blessing to others. And what was Abraham's blessing? Ultimately, it was the salvation of the Gentiles! I have a personal relationship with a holy God because of God's blessing upon Abraham.

As we consider the blessings God pours out on our own lives, do we see them as resources to hoard or opportunities to steward? When God allows something into our lives, for better or for worse, do we stop to ask, "How might I use this blessing to bring glory to God?"

For Abraham, his name is forever connected with the blessing of our salvation. What might the Father do through us if we receive our own blessings with open hands?

We do the works,
but God works in us
in the doing of the works.

—

St. Augustine

Sharing Our Blessings

Jesus never asks us to give Him what we don't have. But He does demand that we give Him all we do have if we want to be a part of what He wishes to do in the lives of those around us!

Anne Graham Lotz

The most eloquent prayer is the prayer through hands that heal and bless. The highest form of worship is the worship of unselfish Christian service. The greatest form of praise is the sound of consecrated feet seeking out the lost and helpless.

Billy Graham

We worship God through service. The authentic server views each opportunity to lead or serve as an opportunity to worship God.

Bill Hybels

Christianity, in its purest form, is nothing more than seeing Jesus. Christian service, in its purest form, is nothing more than imitating him who we see. To see his Majesty and to imitate him: that is the sum of Christianity.

Max Lucado

More from God's Word About Serving Others

The greatest among you will be your servant. For whoever exalts himself will be humbled, and whoever humbles himself will be exalted.

Matthew 23:11-12 NIV

Each of you should look not only to your own interests, but also to the interest of others.

Philippians 2:4 NIV

The one who blesses others is abundantly blessed; those who help others are helped.

Proverbs 11:25 MSG

Be devoted to one another in brotherly love. Honor one another above yourselves.

Romans 12:10 NIV

But whosoever will be great among you, let him be your minister; and whosoever will be chief among you, let him be your servant: even as the Son of man came not to be ministered unto, but to minister, and to give his life a ransom for many.

Matthew 20:26-28 KJV

How Can You Be a Blessing Today?

Even if you're experiencing tough times right now, you still have blessings to count and blessings to share. So ask yourself this question: How can I glorify God today?

Your Heavenly Father has given you talents and opportunities that are uniquely yours. And the very best day to seize those opportunities—and to share them with the world—is this day. Not tomorrow. Not next week. Not next year. Today.

Summing Things Up

God wants you to serve Him now, not later. Don't put off until tomorrow the good works you can perform today.

Your Own Thoughts

CHAPTER 2

THE GREATEST BLESSING

*And you He made alive, who were dead in trespasses
and sins . . . . But God, who is rich in mercy, because of
His great love with which He loved us, even when we were
dead in trespasses, made us alive together with Christ
(by grace you have been saved) . . . .*

Ephesians 2:1, 4-5 NKJV

In Genesis, we learned that God blessed Abraham despite any merit of his own. But, does that offer stand for the rest of us?

May of us believe (wrongly) that we're unworthy of God's love. It's not only that we see ourselves as having little or nothing worth giving Him; it's that we have so many things to apologize to Him for. It's not only that we have little to offer of merit; it's that we have so much to offer that is the antithesis of merit! It's not only that our life histories are woefully short of good deeds; it's that our histories are so full of bad deeds.

We have secrets in our past, things we would be embarrassed to even speak of. We have chronic hang-ups, things that make us feel unable to lead righteous lives. Why, we ask ourselves, would God ever bless someone like me? The answer to this question is the very crux of the gospel.

> We're not only saved by grace, but the Bible says we're sustained by grace.
> —Bill Hybels

The apostle Paul, writer of Ephesians, puts it plainly: "We were dead." There was nothing we could offer to earn the blessing of salvation. Yet, we were in such desperate need of redemption that God, being rich in mercy, showed us His love by sending Jesus to our rescue.

The second chapter of Ephesians tells of the blessings that result from salvation through Christ: We were once far off, yet now have been brought near (v. 13); we were once strangers, but now we are citizens in God's household (v. 19). And, Ephesians 2 also teaches us that God has not only saved us, but that He has also planned good works for us (v. 10).

The blessings described in Ephesians 2 are priceless gifts. There is nothing we could ever do to earn them. We are blessed simply because we are His!

Grace is not about finishing last or first;
it is about not counting.
We receive grace as a gift from God,
not as something we toil to earn.

—

Philip Yancey

About God's Grace

The grace of God means something like: Here is your life. You might never have been, but you are because the party wouldn't have been complete without you. Here is the world. Beautiful and terrible things will happen. Don't be afraid. I am with you. Nothing can ever separate us. It's for you I created the universe. I love you.

Frederick Buechner

How beautiful it is to learn that grace isn't fragile, and that in the family of God we can fail and not be a failure.

Gloria Gaither

You don't earn grace, and you don't deserve grace; you simply receive it as God's loving gift, and then share it with others.

Warren Wiersbe

Grace and gratitude belong together like heaven and earth. Grace evokes gratitude like the voice of an echo. Gratitude follows grace as thunder follows lightning.

Karl Barth

The Gospel is not so much a demand as it is an offer, an offer of new life to man by the grace of God.

E. Stanley Jones

More from God's Word About
Gifts from the Father

The LORD is my strength and song, and He has become my salvation; He is my God, and I will praise Him . . . .

Exodus 15:2 NKJV

But my God shall supply all your need according to his riches in glory by Christ Jesus.

Philippians 4:19 KJV

The Lord is my rock, my fortress and my savior; my God is my rock in whom I find protection. He is my shield, the strength of my salvation, and my stronghold.

Psalm 18:2 NLT

The Lord says, "I will rescue those who love me. I will protect those who trust in my name."

Psalm 91:14 NLT

Therefore, since we are receiving a kingdom that cannot be shaken, let us hold on to grace. By it, we may serve God acceptably, with reverence and awe.

Hebrews 12:28 HCSB

Eternal Gifts

Here's a question worth pondering: What blessings are you receiving today, and how will those blessings affect the way you choose to live your life?

Even on our most difficult days, we are surrounded by God's love. Yet, we sometimes focus so intently on our earthly disappointments that we fail to recognize God's eternal gifts.

Today, consider what the greatest blessing—God's gift of grace—means to you. And, while you're at it, consider ways you can nourish that gift and share it.

Summing Things Up

By God's grace we are saved, and by God's grace we live each day. God's grace is an incredible gift, a priceless blessing to be treasured and shared.

Your Own Thoughts

CHAPTER 3

WE PRAY FOR BLESSINGS, BUT WHAT KIND?

☙

For now we see indistinctly, as in a mirror,
but then face to face.
Now I know in part, but then I will know fully,
as I am fully known.

—

1 Corinthians 13:12 HCSB

When you pray for blessings, what kind do you pray for? If you're like most of us, you probably pray for things like health, wealth, and safety for yourself and for your loved ones. And, if you're like most of us, you're probably disappointed if God doesn't give you the things you've asked for.

Because we're only here on earth for a few short years at best, we human beings have a decidedly short-term perspective. Usually, we pray for the blessings that we believe will improve our lives today, or tomorrow, or next week, or next year. But, God has an eternal perspective—He sees His creation (and we're all part of that creation) in the context of eternity.

Time and again, the Bible teaches us that God is sovereign and that He reigns over His creation. Our Heavenly Father has a plan for the world and for our lives. He does not do things by accident, but we cannot always understand His purposes. Why? Because we are mortal beings with limited understanding. And although we cannot fully comprehend the will of God, we should always do our best to trust the will of God even when we don't receive the things we've prayed for.

Grace grows best
in the winter.

—

C. H. Spurgeon

About Unanswered Prayers

Prayer is request. The essence of request, as distinct from compulsion, is that it may or may not be granted. And if an infinitely wise being listens to the requests of finite and foolish creatures, of course He will sometimes grant and sometimes refuse them.

C. S. Lewis

If God chooses to remain silent, faith is content.

Ruth Bell Graham

Our Lord never asks us to decide for Him; He asks us to yield to Him—a very different matter.

Oswald Chambers

Prayer may not get us what we want, but it will teach us to want what we need.

Vance Havner

We must meet our disappointments, our persecutions, our malicious enemies, our provoking friends, our trials and temptations of every sort, with an attitude of surrender and trust. We must spread our wings and "mount up" to the "heavenly places in Christ" above them all, where they will lose their power to harm or distress us.

Hannah Whitall Smith

More from God's Word About
His Infinite Wisdom and Power

Can you solve the mysteries of God? Can you discover everything there is to know about the Almighty? Such knowledge is higher than the heavens—but who are you? It is deeper than the underworld—what can you know in comparison to him? It is broader than the earth and wider than the sea.

Job 11:7-9 NLT

The earth and everything in it, the world and its inhabitants, belong to the Lord.

Psalm 24:1 HCSB

Should we accept only good from God and not adversity?
Job 2:10 HCSB

"For my thoughts are not your thoughts, neither are your ways my ways," declares the LORD. "As the heavens are higher than the earth, so are my ways higher than your ways and my thoughts than your thoughts."

Isaiah 55:8-9 NIV

We can gather our thoughts, but the LORD gives the right answer. People may be pure in their own eyes, but the LORD examines their motives.

Proverbs 16:1-2 NLT

Learning the Art of Acceptance

When events transpire that are beyond our control, we have a clear choice: we can either learn the art of acceptance, or we can make ourselves miserable as we struggle to change the unchangeable.

Learning the art of acceptance is difficult for most of us, but not impossible. Can you summon the courage and the wisdom to accept life on its own terms? Can you do it today?

Surrender to the Lord is not a tremendous sacrifice,
not an agonizing performance.
It is the most sensible thing you can do.

—

Corrie ten Boom

Summing Things Up

Sometimes, the blessings God gives us are not the ones we've asked for. But even when we cannot understand God's plan for our lives, we should be thankful for His eternal perspective and His eternal love.

Your Own Thoughts

CHAPTER 4

WHAT IF YOUR BLESSINGS COME THROUGH RAINDROPS?

God blesses the people who patiently endure testing.
Afterward they will receive the crown of life that
God has promised to those who love him.

—

James 1:12 NLT

Have you ever experienced a bitter disappointment—or even a personal tragedy—that later turned out to be a blessing? Have you ever experienced a temporary loss that, in time, was transformed into a permanent gain? And, do you believe that God has the power to use all your experiences—the good, the bad, and the in-between—for His purposes? If you answered "yes" to one or more of these questions, then you know that blessings can, and often do, come through raindrops.

In times of hardship and pain, we may feel abandoned by our friends, by our families, and by our Creator. But if we believe that God has left us, even for a moment, we are mistaken. God never abandons us, not even when the raindrops are falling in buckets. Through every storm of life, He is ever-present, offering us His grace, His love, and His mercies.

When Jesus went to the Mount of Olives, He prayed, "Father, if it is Your will, take this cup away from Me; nevertheless not My will, but Yours, be done" (Luke 22:42). Jesus knew the pain that He was destined to endure, but He also knew that God's will must be done.

> God uses every cloud which comes in our physical life, in our moral or spiritual life, or in our circumstances, to bring us nearer to him until we come to the place where our Lord Jesus Christ lived, and we do not allow our hearts to be troubled.
> —Oswald Chambers

From time to time all of us must endure days filled with suffering and heartache. And, as human beings with limited understanding, we can never fully understand God's reasons for allowing the raindrops to fall. But, even when we cannot understand why things happen as they do, we should always trust the One who is intent upon blessing us throughout all eternity.

Can you trust God in times of happiness and in times of hardship? Can you trust Him today?

Rejoice in hope; be patient in affliction; be persistent in prayer.

—

Romans 12:12 HCSB

About Tough Times

If we believe in Jesus Christ, we can face every problem that the world holds.

Oswald Chambers

Jesus loved the will of His Father. He embraced the limitations, the necessities, the conditions, the very chains of his humanity as he walked and worked here on earth, fulfilling moment by moment His divine commission and the stern demands of His incarnation. Never was there a word or even a look of complaint.

Elisabeth Elliot

Through all of the crises of life—and we all are going to experience them—we have this magnificent Anchor.

Franklin Graham

Sometimes the Lord rides out the storm with us and other times He calms the restless sea around us. Most of all, He calms the storm inside us in our deepest inner soul.

Lloyd John Ogilvie

Contentment is trusting God even when things seem out of control.

Charles Stanley

Teach us to set our hopes
on heaven, to hold firmly
to the promise of eternal life,
so that we can withstand the
struggles and storms of this world.

—
Max Lucado

More from God's Word About Adversity

We are pressured in every way but not crushed; we are perplexed but not in despair.

2 Corinthians 4:8 HCSB

You have allowed me to suffer much hardship, but you will restore me to life again and lift me up from the depths of the earth. You will restore me to even greater honor and comfort me once again.

Psalm 71:20-21 NLT

Blessed is he whose help is the God of Jacob, whose hope is in the LORD his God, the Maker of heaven and earth, the sea, and everything in them—the LORD, who remains faithful forever.

Psalm 146:5-6 NIV

Summing Things Up

When raindrops begin to fall and hope begins to fade, we can be sure that God's love remains. And, we can be sure that His blessings do, at times, come through raindrops.

Your Own Thoughts

CHAPTER 5

WHEN FAITH DISAPPEARS

*Immediately the father of the child cried out and said
with tears, "Lord, I believe; help my unbelief!"*

—

Mark 9:24 NKJV

Have you ever become so discouraged by life's hardships that you felt your faith in God slipping away? If so, you are not alone. Every life—including yours—is a series of celebrations and disappointments, joys and sorrows, successes and failures, hopes and doubts. Even the most faithful men and women may be overcome by bouts of fear and doubt, and so, perhaps, will you.

Doubts come in several flavors: doubts about God, doubts about the future, and doubts about your own abilities, for starters. So what does the Bible say about your response to these kinds of doubts? The Bible makes it clear that no problem in this world is too big for God, not even the problems that result from the emotional burdens of fear and doubt.

The instructions of Psalm 55:22 are clear: "Cast your burden on the Lord, and He shall sustain you; He shall never permit the righteous to be moved" (NKJV). Will you cast your burdens on the Lord? Will you take your doubts to Him? Your fears? Your sorrows? Your setbacks and regrets? Will you take these things to Him—and leave them there—today?

> The only way to learn a strong faith is to endure great trials. We learn faith by standing firm amid the most severe of tests.
> —George Mueller

When Doubts Creep In

I was learning something important: we are most vulnerable to the piercing winds of doubt when we distance ourselves from the mission and fellowship to which Christ has called us. Our night of discouragement will seem endless and our task impossible, unless we recognize that He stands in our midst.

Joni Eareckson Tada

Struggling with God over the issues of life doesn't show a lack of faith—that is faith.

Lee Strobel

Some people feel guilty about their anxieties and regard them as a defect of faith, but they are afflictions, not sins. Like all afflictions, they are, if we can so take them, our share in the passion of Christ.

C. S. Lewis

There is a difference between doubt and unbelief. Doubt is a matter of mind: we cannot understand what God is doing or why He is doing it. Unbelief is a matter of will: we refuse to believe God's Word and obey what He tells us to do.

Warren Wiersbe

God is the only one
who can make the valley of
trouble a door of hope.

—

Catherine Marshall

More from God's Word About Overcoming Fear

Don't be afraid, because I am your God. I will make you strong and will help you; I will support you with my right hand that saves you.

Isaiah 41:10 NCV

Don't be afraid, because the Lord your God will be with you everywhere you go.

Joshua 1:9 NCV

Be strong and courageous, and do the work. Do not be afraid or discouraged, for the Lord God, my God, is with you.

1 Chronicles 28:20 NIV

The Lord is my light and my salvation; whom shall I fear? The Lord is the strength of my life; of whom shall I be afraid?

Psalm 27:1 KJV

I sought the LORD, and he answered me; he delivered me from all my fears.

Psalm 34:4 NIV

One Thing Is Certain

Some things in life are uncertain: health may vanish; wealth may disappear; success may be fleeting, and the victories we hold most dear may, in time, be transformed into bitter defeats. But in a world of uncertainties, one thing is certain: God loves us. And that one fact can make all the difference.

Summing Things Up

When doubts creep in, as they will from time to time, remember that God isn't just near, He's here . . . and He's ready to talk to you right now.

Your Own Thoughts

CHAPTER 6

THE BLESSING OF COMING AS WE ARE

But I trust in your unfailing love;
my heart rejoices in your salvation.
I will sing the LORD's praise,
for he has been good to me.

—

Psalm 13:5-6 NIV

How long, O LORD? Will You forget me forever?
How long will You hide Your face from me?
How long shall I take counsel in my soul,
Having sorrow in my heart all the day?
How long will my enemy be exalted over me?
Consider and answer me, O LORD my God;
Enlighten my eyes, or I will sleep the sleep of death,
And my enemy will say, "I have overcome him,"
And my adversaries will rejoice when I am shaken.
But I have trusted in Your lovingkindness;
My heart shall rejoice in Your salvation.
I will sing to the LORD,
Because He has dealt bountifully with me.

—

Psalm 13 NASB

Psalm 13 has become one of my favorite passages. As I reflect on the words of David, I am reminded of one unique blessing: A holy and perfect God invites us to come as we are. King David was very honest before the Lord with his feelings, "How long O Lord? Will You forget me forever?"

When I am honest with myself, I can relate to David's sentiments. So often I feel forgotten by God. Was his head turned when my husband's brain tumor slipped into our lives? How could He have let this happen?

The good news is this: While we may not understand the ways of the Lord, He bids us to come to Him with our frustrations and doubts. When we feel that He has deserted us, we can tell Him. When life seems too hard, He longs for us to bring Him our burdens.

In the midst of David's brutal honesty, he doesn't end with the things he feels. David ends by stating what He knows. David knows that we cannot allow our emotions to reign over our lives. And, he knows that we must be grounded by the truth of God.

> That's what I love about serving God. In His eyes, there are no little people . . . because there are no big people. We are all on the same playing field. We all start at square one. No one has it better than the other, or possesses unfair advantage.
> —*Joni Eareckson Tada*

David concludes Psalm 13 by proclaiming, "But I have trusted in Your loving kindness." With this statement, David chooses to put his full weight on the sturdy foundation of God's love. Though he may feel deserted, David chooses to trust God. Though his life may feel purposeless, David trusts that God still has a plan and is still reigning over the chaos.

Lastly, David chooses to sing. Will we chose to sing today, or will we merely bring our complaints to God? May God birth in our hearts a song to carry us through the day, for He has truly dealt bountifully with us!

God loves us the way we are,
but He loves us too much
to leave us that way.

—

Leighton Ford

About God's Love

Being loved by Him whose opinion matters most gives us the security to risk loving, too—even loving ourselves.

Gloria Gaither

If you can forgive the person you were, accept the person you are, and believe in the person you will become, you are headed for joy. So celebrate your life.

Barbara Johnson

Believing that you are loved will set you free to be who God created you to be. So rest in His love and just be yourself.

Lisa Whelchel

Our Savior kneels down and gazes upon the darkest acts of our lives. But rather than recoil in horror, he reaches out in kindness and says, "I can clean that if you want." And from the basin of his grace, he scoops a palm full of mercy and washes our sin.

Max Lucado

God loves each of us as if there were only one of us.

St. Augustine

*For God loved the world
in this way:
He gave His only Son,
so that everyone who believes
in Him will not perish
but have eternal life.*

—

John 3:16 HCSB

More from God's Word About the Father's Love

For the Lord is good, and His love is eternal; His faithfulness endures through all generations.

Psalm 100:5 HCSB

[Because of] the Lord's faithful love we do not perish, for His mercies never end. They are new every morning; great is Your faithfulness!

Lamentations 3:22-23 HCSB

Help me, Lord my God; save me according to Your faithful love.

Psalm 109:26 HCSB

Whoever is wise will observe these things, and they will understand the lovingkindness of the Lord.

Psalm 107:43 NKJV

Summing Things Up

Despite our imperfections, God invites us to come as we are. And, despite our lack of faith, God's love for us never waivers. His faithfulness endures forever.

Your Own Thoughts

CHAPTER 7

THE BLESSING OF GOD'S PURSUING LOVE

Then I will go to the altar of God,
to God my exceeding joy;
and upon the lyre I shall praise You, O God, my God.

—

Psalm 43:4 NASB

Vindicate me, O God, and plead my case against
an ungodly nation;
O deliver me from the deceitful and unjust man!
For You are the God of my strength;
why have You rejected me?
Why do I go mourning because of the oppression
of the enemy?
O send out Your light and Your truth, let them lead me;
Let them bring me to Your holy hill
And to Your dwelling places.
Then I will go to the altar of God,
To God my exceeding joy;
And upon the lyre I shall praise You, O God, my God.
Why are you in despair, O my soul?
And why are you disturbed within me?
Hope in God, for I shall again praise Him,
The help of my countenance and my God.

—

Psalm 43 NIV

One of the greatest blessings of God's love is His consistent pursuit. It is a supernatural love like none we have ever known. It's a love that never slows down, never falters, and never stops.

As a worship leader, it's embarrassing to admit that there are days that I don't feel like worshiping. Maybe I'm too tired, too busy, or just in a bad mood. Maybe I have done something that is displeasing to God, and I am too ashamed to even approach Him. Yet, as Psalm 43 explains, my job is to just call on His name.

> The life of faith is a daily exploration of the constant and countless ways in which God's grace and love are experienced.
> —*Eugene Peterson*

God has enlisted His marvelous light and soul-piercing truth to come to us, take us by the hand, and to lead us to that place of worship.

When I cannot remember the way to God, He will lead me. When I do not have the strength to search for Him, He still pursues my soul!

About Trusting God

God's love is measureless. It is more: it is boundless. It has no bounds because it is not a thing but a facet of the essential nature of God. His love is something he is, and because he is infinite, that love can enfold the whole created world in itself and have room for ten thousand times ten thousand worlds beside.

A. W. Tozer

As we stand at the Cross of Christ, we see a glorious exhibition of God's love.

Billy Graham

God is not hurried along in the Time-stream of this universe any more than an author is hurried along in the imaginary time of his own novel. He has infinite attention to spare for each one of us. He does not have to deal with us in the mass. You are as much alone with Him as if you were the only being He had ever created. When Christ died, He died for you individually just as much as if you have been the only man in the world.

C. S. Lewis

Faith is unutterable trust in God, trust which never dreams that He will not stand by us.

Oswald Chambers

It was not the soldiers
who killed him,
nor the screams of the mob:
It was his devotion to us.

—

Max Lucado

More from God's Word About His Mercy

Praise be to the God and Father of our Lord Jesus Christ! In his great mercy he has given us new birth into a living hope through the resurrection of Jesus Christ from the dead....

1 Peter 1:3 NIV

But because of his great love for us, God, who is rich in mercy, made us alive with Christ even when we were dead in transgressions — it is by grace you have been saved.

Ephesians 2:4-5 NIV

O praise the LORD, all ye nations: praise him, all ye people. For his merciful kindness is great toward us: and the truth of the LORD endureth for ever. Praise ye the LORD.

Psalm 117 KJV

Summing Things Up

God's love is a pursuing love; He never abandons us. And when we are lost, God will lead us back to Himself if we let Him.

Your Own Thoughts

CHAPTER 8

WHEN WE LOSE THE SENSE OF HIS NEARNESS

Draw near to God, and He will draw near to you.

—

James 4:8 HCSB

Sometimes life can be so full of craziness and stress that we lose the sense of God's nearness. But even when we feel alienated from the Father, He is never alienated from us. Whenever we think God has moved away from us, we are mistaken; He hasn't moved at all.

God is constantly making Himself available to us, but when we become overwhelmed by the occasional distractions or inevitable disappointments of everyday life, we may be unwilling—or unable—to feel His presence or His love.

> Whatever hallway you're in—no matter how long, how dark, or how scary—God is right there with you.
> —*Bill Hybels*

The next time you feel overwhelmed by the demands of life, remember that our God isn't a distant God. He is always present; His love for you is personal, intimate, and eternal. If you genuinely desire to open your heart to the Creator, you can do so because He is not just near; He is here.

God walks with us.
He scoops us up in His arms
or simply sits with us in silent
strength until we cannot avoid
the awesome recognition that yes,
even now, He is here.

—

Gloria Gaither

God Is Always Near

We need never shout across the spaces to an absent God. He is nearer than our own soul, closer than our most secret thoughts.

A. W. Tozer

Let this be your chief object in prayer: to realize the presence of your heavenly Father. Let your watchword be: Alone with God.

Andrew Murray

Certainly, God is with us in times of distress, and that is a comforting truth. But listen: Jesus wants to be part of every experience and every moment of our lives.

Billy Graham

As sure as God puts his children in the furnace, he will be in the furnace with them.

C. H. Spurgeon

The real test of being in the presence of God is that you either forget about yourself altogether or see yourself as a very small object. It is better to forget about yourself altogether.

C. S. Lewis

More from God's Word About the Father's Presence

You will seek Me and find Me when you search for Me with all your heart.

Jeremiah 29:13 HCSB

The Lord is near all who call out to Him, all who call out to Him with integrity. He fulfills the desires of those who fear Him; He hears their cry for help and saves them.

Psalm 145:18-19 HCSB

Surely goodness and mercy shall follow me all the days of my life; and I will dwell in the house of the Lord for ever.

Psalm 23:6 KJV

I am not alone, because the Father is with Me.

John 16:32 HCSB

Fear not, for I am with you; be not dismayed, for I am your God. I will strengthen you.

Isaiah 41:10 NKJV

The Lord is with you when you are with Him. If you seek Him, He will be found by you.

2 Chronicles 15:2 HCSB

Putting on the Armor of God

In a world filled with dangers and temptations, God is the ultimate armor. In a world filled with misleading messages, God's Word is the ultimate truth. In a world filled with more frustrations than we can count, God's Son offers the ultimate peace. Will you accept God's peace and wear God's armor against the dangers of our world?

Sometimes, in the crush of everyday life, God may seem far away, but He is not. God is everywhere you have ever been and everywhere you will ever go. He is with you night and day; He knows your thoughts and your prayers. He is your ultimate Protector. And, when you earnestly seek His protection, you will find it because He is here—always—waiting patiently for you to reach out to Him.

Summing Things Up

Even when we feel alienated from God, He is never alienated from us. God walks with us through every phase of life, through every trial and hardship. Despite our doubts and fears, He is always with us.

Your Own Thoughts

CHAPTER 9

OUR BLESSED HOPE

*For the grace of God that brings salvation has appeared
to all men, teaching us that, denying ungodliness and
worldly lusts, we should live soberly, righteously,
and godly in the present age, looking for the blessed hope
and glorious appearing of our great God and Savior
Jesus Christ, who gave Himself for us, that He might
redeem us from every lawless deed and purify for Himself
His own special people, zealous for good works.*

—

Titus 2:11-14 NKJV

We lead not-so-perfect lives, and we inhabit a less-than-ideal world. Things go wrong, people misbehave, bad things happen, and hope is sometimes in short supply. But even when life seems to be spinning out of control, we still have every reason to be optimistic about our futures. Why? Because we are loved and protected by the Creator of the universe, that's why.

One of my favorite quotations comes from the author and theologian C. S. Lewis, who observed, "If I find in myself a desire which no experience in this world can satisfy, the most probable explanation is that I was made for another world." This quotation reminds me that it's okay for my life to be less than fulfilling. In fact, it's entirely possible that my deepest desires for physical, relational, and emotional healing are being intentionally left unmet in order to point me toward something that's far greater.

There is joy to be found in this life through Jesus Christ; yet, He will not let our joy be complete here on this earth. Any sense of wholeness we feel is simply an appetizer. Any display of splendor on this earth is simply the opening act for His "glorious appearing."

> And because we know Christ is alive, we have hope for the present and hope for life beyond the grave.
> —*Billy Graham*

Is it possible that God leaves an ache in my soul to remind me that this is not my home? Does He leave that tinge there to impassion me to tell others about that hope?

This is our blessed hope: that we are His and will someday spend eternity with Him. Until then, we are strangers and foreigners, left with the scars, and the limps, and all the other subtle reminders of that sweet truth: we are not yet home.

Teach us to set our hopes
on heaven, to hold firmly
to the promise of eternal life,
so that we can withstand the
struggles and storms of this world.

—

Max Lucado

The Blessed Hope of Eternal Life

God has promised us abundance, peace, and eternal life. These treasures are ours for the asking; all we must do is claim them. One of the great mysteries of life is why on earth do so many of us wait so very long to lay claim to God's gifts?

Marie T. Freeman

I can still hardly believe it. I, with shriveled, bent fingers, atrophied muscles, gnarled knees, and no feeling from the shoulders down, will one day have a new body— light, bright and clothed in righteousness—powerful and dazzling.

Joni Eareckson Tada

God dwells in eternity, but time dwells in God. He has already lived all our tomorrows as he has lived all our yesterdays.

A. W. Tozer

The damage done to us on this earth will never find its way into that safe city. We can relax, we can rest, and though some of us can hardly imagine it, we can prepare to feel safe and secure for all of eternity.

Bill Hybels

The unfolding of our friendship with the Father will be a never-ending revelation stretching on into eternity.

Catherine Marshall

More from God's Word About Hope

*Let us hold on to the confession of our hope without wavering,
for He who promised is faithful.*

Hebrews 10:23 HCSB

Hope deferred makes the heart sick.

Proverbs 13:12 NKJV

*Sustain me as You promised, and I will live; do not let me be
ashamed of my hope.*

Psalm 119:116 HCSB

*Be of good courage, and He shall strengthen your heart, all
you who hope in the Lord.*

Psalm 31:24 NKJV

Summing Things Up

We have a blessed hope: that we will spend eternity
with our Father in heaven. But until then, we remain
strangers and foreigners here on earth, reminded
constantly of the bittersweet truth that we are not
yet home.

Your Own Thoughts

CHAPTER 10

WHEN STRENGTH IS GONE

I cried out to the Lord in my suffering, and he heard me.
He set me free from all my fears.

—

Psalm 34:6 NLT

At times, even the strongest among us run out of energy. The demands of daily life can drain us of our strength and rob us of the joy that is rightfully ours in Christ. When we find ourselves tired, discouraged, or worse, there is a source from which we can draw the power needed to recharge our spiritual batteries. That source, of course, is God.

The missionary Andrew Murray observed, "Where there is much prayer, there will be much of the Spirit; where there is much of the Spirit, there will be ever increasing power." These words remind us that the ultimate source of our strength is God. When we turn to Him—for guidance, for wisdom, and for strength—we will not be disappointed.

> He is the same yesterday, today, and forever, and His unchanging and unfailing love sustains me when nothing and no one else can.
> —Bill Bright

Do you need renewal? Is your energy on the wane? Are your emotions frayed? If so, take the time—or, more accurately, make the time—to delve deeply into God's Holy Word. Are you spiritually depleted? Call upon friends and family to support you, and call upon Christ to renew your spirit and your life. When you do, you'll discover that the Creator of the universe has the power to make all things new . . . including you.

Finding Strength

Our valleys may be filled with foes and tears, but we can lift our eyes to the hills to see God and the angels.

Billy Graham

Though our feelings come and go, God's love for us does not.

C. S. Lewis

Are you a Christian? If you are, how can you be hopeless? Are you so depressed by the greatness of your problems that you have given up all hope? Instead of giving up, would you patiently endure? Would you focus on Christ until you are so preoccupied with him alone that you fall prostrate before him?

Anne Graham Lotz

God's all-sufficiency is a major. Your inability is a minor. Major in majors, not in minors.

Corrie ten Boom

Give your cares to Him who cares for the flowers of the field. Rest assured He will also care for you.

C. H. Spurgeon

Just remember,
every flower that ever bloomed
had to go through a whole lot
of dirt to get there!

—

Barbara Johnson

More from God's Word About Strength

And He said to me, "My grace is sufficient for you, for My strength is made perfect in weakness."

2 Corinthians 12:9 NKJV

He gives strength to the weary and strengthens the powerless.

Isaiah 40:29 HCSB

Finally, be strengthened by the Lord and by His vast strength.

Ephesians 6:10 HCSB

You, therefore, my child, be strong in the grace that is in Christ Jesus.

2 Timothy 2:1 HCSB

The Lord is my strength and my song; He has become my salvation.

Exodus 15:2 HCSB

Pray for Strength

Where do you turn for strength? Do you depend upon the world's promises or, for that matter, upon your own resources? Or do you turn toward God for the wisdom and strength to meet the challenges of the coming day? The answer should be obvious: God comes first.

Each morning, before you become caught up in the complexities of everyday life, spend meaningful moments with your Creator. Offer Him your prayers and study His Word. When you offer God the firstfruits of your day, you gain wisdom, perspective, and strength.

Summing Things Up

Whatever your need, God can provide. When you are tired, fearful, or discouraged, God can restore your strength.

Your Own Thoughts

CHAPTER 11

THE BLESSINGS THAT THE WORLD HAS TO OFFER

The Lord was very angry with Solomon,
for his heart had turned away from the Lord,
the God of Israel, who had appeared to him twice.
He had warned Solomon specifically about worshiping
other gods, but Solomon did not listen
to the Lord's command.

—

1 Kings 11:9-10 NLT

If you're like me, you've heard a lot about the "American Dream." You know the dream I'm talking about; it's the one that says if you work hard enough, know the right people, and say the right things, you can somehow obtain the nice house, the right car, the white picket fence, and the 2.5 kids. But, is this really the dream God has for us? And, if it's not part of God's plans for us, are we selling ourselves short by sacrificing so much for a "dream" that offers us little or nothing in return?

King Solomon also started with a dream. As a part of his dream, Solomon was able to ask God for anything—and what he asked for was wisdom. "Give your servant an understanding heart to judge Your people to discern between good and evil."

> The more we stuff ourselves with material pleasures, the less we seem to appreciate life.
> —*Barbara Johnson*

Like Abraham, Solomon asked God to bless Him with wisdom so that he might, in turn, bless the nation of Israel. God granted Solomon's request, and peace and prosperity was enjoyed throughout Israel.

Eventually, Solomon's desire for the blessing of wisdom changed. What happened? King Solomon became trapped by a powerful temptation: the temptation to accumulate things. It began when Solomon acquired alliances with other nations; then, he acquired enormous wealth and many, many women (around a thousand to be exact). To make matters worse, Solomon built a large palace for himself (that palace, by the way, just happened to be twice as large as the one he had constructed for the Lord to dwell in). Amazed at how "blessed" Solomon was, the queen of Sheba even traveled to visit him.

But what did these earthly treasures bring Solomon? The answer, not surprisingly, is trouble. We are told that Solomon's "wives turned his heart away to other Gods" (1 Kings 11:4). Could it be that Solomon had elevated those beautiful creations above their Creator? Is it possible that Solomon began to worship the blessings, rather than the Giver of the blessings? Solomon had the resources to procure every possession his heart desired, and yet those very possessions were his downfall.

And what about the rest of us? Have we bought into the lie that if we had just a little more money, we'd be satisfied? Or, do we believe that if we had different spouses, or that if we were from different families, or that if we had different jobs, then we would be blessed?

When I see how greedy my own heart is, I am reminded that the worst thing God could do for me is to give me the very treasures I have elevated above Him. The blessings of this world will never satisfy. Though scripture tells us that every good and perfect gift comes from the Lord, unless they stay surrendered to the Giver, those blessings have the potential to become little idols, stealing away the attention and affection that we should give to God alone.

It's sobering to contemplate
how much time, effort,
sacrifice, compromise, and
attention we give to acquiring
and increasing our supply
of something that is totally
insignificant in eternity.

Anne Graham Lotz

The Dangers of Materialism

If you want to be truly happy, you won't find it on an endless quest for more stuff. You'll find it in receiving God's generosity and then passing that generosity along.

Bill Hybels

Greed is evil because it substitutes material things for the place of honor that the Creator ought to have in an individual's life.

Charles Stanley

Greed is enslaving. The more you have, the more you want—until eventually avarice consumes you.

Kay Arthur

Why is love of gold more potent than love of souls?

Lottie Moon

A society that pursues pleasure runs the risk of raising expectations ever higher, so that true contentment always lies tantalizingly out of reach.

Philip Yancey and Paul Brand

More from God's Word About Greed

Do not love the world or the things in the world. If anyone loves the world, the love of the Father is not in him.

1 John 2:15 NKJV

For the love of money is a root of all sorts of evil, and some by longing for it have wandered away from the faith and pierced themselves with many griefs. But flee from these things, you man of God, and pursue righteousness, godliness, faith, love, perseverance and gentleness.

1 Timothy 6:11 NASB

Your life should be free from the love of money. Be satisfied with what you have, for He Himself has said, I will never leave you or forsake you.

Hebrews 13:5 HCSB

When the Passover Feast, celebrated each spring by the Jews, was about to take place, Jesus traveled up to Jerusalem. He found the Temple teeming with people selling cattle and sheep and doves. The loan sharks were also there in full strength. Jesus put together a whip out of strips of leather and chased them out of the Temple, stampeding the sheep and cattle, upending the tables of the loan sharks, spilling coins left and right. He told the dove merchants, "Get your things out of here! Stop turning my Father's house into a shopping mall!"

John 2:13-16 MSG

Worshipping God, Not Mankind

Lord, forgive us when we mistakenly worship the "American Dream" instead of You. In good times and hard times, let us seek the eternal blessings You give, not the earthly blessings that the world promises but cannot deliver. And, let us receive whatever You offer us with open hands, knowing that You give things—and take things away—for our good.

Summing Things Up

Material possessions may seem appealing at first, but they pale in comparison to the spiritual gifts that God gives to those who put Him first. Count yourself among that number.

Your Own Thoughts

CHAPTER 12

HE LOVES US TOO MUCH TO GIVE US LESSER THINGS

*For I am persuaded that neither death nor life,
nor angels nor rulers, nor things present, nor things to
come, nor powers, nor height, nor depth, nor any other
created thing will have the power to separate us from
the love of God that is in Christ Jesus our Lord!*

—

Romans 8:38-39 HCSB

If God loves us, why does He seemingly withhold His blessings, especially when we're weak or vulnerable? That question has no easy answer. After all, none of us can understand why God does the things He does. But, I'm convinced that the things we sometimes see as senseless suffering are often blessings in disguise.

God sees the entire landscape of our lives from an eternal perspective, and He knows, far better than we ever could, the value of His grace. God loves us intimately and individually. He loves us too much to offer us lesser gifts, gifts that might somehow distance our hearts from Him.

Have you been troubled by a setback you simply cannot understand? If so, try spending less time asking "why" and more time thinking about God's love for you. His love is infinite and eternal. It's surrounding you right now. Accept it and be grateful.

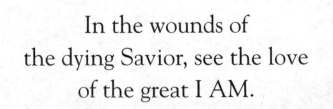

In the wounds of
the dying Savior, see the love
of the great I AM.

—

C. H. Spurgeon

God Loves and Protects Us

He can give only according to His might; therefore he always gives more than we ask for.

Martin Luther

The stars may fall, but God's promises will stand and be fulfilled.

J. I. Packer

Kept by His power—that is the only safety.

Oswald Chambers

Only believe, don't fear. Our Master, Jesus, always watches over us, and no matter what the persecution, Jesus will surely overcome it.

Lottie Moon

We have ample evidence that the Lord is able to guide. The promises cover every imaginable situation. All we need to do is to take the hand he stretches out.

Elisabeth Elliot

God does not give us everything we want, but He does fulfill all His promises as He leads us along the best and straightest paths to Himself.

Dietrich Bonhoeffer

More from God's Word About God's Protection

Every word of God is flawless; he is a shield to those who take refuge in him.

Proverbs 30:5 NIV

I will lift up my eyes to the mountains; from whence shall my help come? My help comes from the Lord, who made the heaven and earth.

Psalm 121:1-2 NASB

Now the God of all grace, who called you to His eternal glory in Christ Jesus, will personally restore, establish, strengthen, and support you.

1 Peter 5:10 HCSB

And my God shall supply all your need according to His riches in glory by Christ Jesus.

Philippians 4:19 NKJV

Celebrating His Love

You know the profound love that you hold in your heart for your family and friends. As a child of God, you can only imagine the infinite love that your Heavenly Father has for you.

Today, what will you do in response to God's love? Will you live purposefully and joyfully? Will you celebrate God's creation while giving thanks for His blessings? And will you share God's love with family members, friends, and even strangers? Hopefully so. After all, God's message—and His love—are meant to be shared.

Summing Things Up

When all else fails, God's love does not. You can always depend upon God's love.

Your Own Thoughts

CHAPTER 13

THE BLESSED THORN

My grace is sufficient for you,
for My strength is made perfect in weakness.

—

2 Corinthians 12:9 NKJV

It's hard to remember what age I was when I was first pricked by a thorn, the moment that I was first stunned by the illusive beauty of a rose. Trying to grasp it, I immediately felt the prick. Such was my introduction to a profound paradox: In the midst of great beauty, there is often real pain.

Paul, in one of his most candid moments in scripture, talked about a thorn that had dug into his flesh. He didn't tell us what that figurative thorn was, but he did admit that it caused him great pain.

Paul also admitted that he pleaded with God, asking Him to take the thorn away, yet the Lord refused to act. Paul prayed for God to ease his pain by altering his circumstances, yet God's answer was a resounding no.

Theologians have speculated for centuries over the nature of Paul's malady, but for me, the real message of this passage lies not in the exact nature of Paul's illness, but in the simple fact that God could have done something, but He chose not to.

Why did God withhold healing from Paul? Was it because God couldn't? I certainly doubt that the Almighty God, the One who parted the Red Sea and delivered Jesus from the grave, would have had any trouble removing

> Extraordinary afflictions are not always the punishment of extraordinary sins, but sometimes the trial of extraordinary graces. Sanctified afflictions are spiritual promotions.
> —*Matthew Henry*

Paul's thorn. But, just because God can do all things, doesn't mean He is obligated to. The only things restraining God's actions are His own character and His own goodness, and His divine purpose.

Another common assumption might be that God left Paul to suffer because Paul deserved it. Prior to becoming a Christian, Paul had actually persecuted and killed those following "the way." Is it possible Paul's "thorn" was simply God's retribution? I don't believe so. Though Paul deserved death, God's Word makes it clear that Jesus paid for Paul's sins on the cross; it's the same sacrifice that Christ has made for you and me.

God's words to Paul come not only as explanation but as comfort as well: "My grace is sufficient for you, for My strength is made perfect in weakness." God left the thorn so that His power could be displayed all the more clearly in Paul's life. In the midst of Paul's struggle, God's grace, all the unmerited peace and strength that Paul would ever need, was always available.

And, the very same grace that gave Paul strength is available to you, right here, right now.

The Thorns of Life

God has never promised to keep us immune from trouble. He says, "I will be with you in trouble."

Oswald Chambers

The beauty of God's Power is that it points people directly back to the source: God Himself.

Bill Hybels

Simply put, our suffering is temporary—just like the bodies in which we are suffering are temporary. But, the rewards we are accumulating while in these temporary bodies are eternal. God has allowed us to participate in a system by which the temporal can be used to gain what is eternal.

Charles Stanley

He is ever faithful and gives us the song in the night to soothe our spirits and fresh joy each morning to lift our souls. What a marvelous Lord!

Bill Bright

God, who foresaw your tribulation, has specially armed you to go through it, not without pain, but without stain.

C. S. Lewis

Jesus Christ is not
a security from storms.
He is perfect security in storms.

—

Kathy Troccoli

More from God's Word About God's Faithfulness

I will sing of the tender mercies of the Lord forever! Young and old will hear of your faithfulness. Your unfailing love will last forever. Your faithfulness is as enduring as the heavens.

Psalm 89:1-2 NLT

God is faithful, by whom you were called into the fellowship of His Son, Jesus Christ our Lord.

1 Corinthians 1:9 NKJV

Because of the LORD'S great love we are not consumed, for his compassions never fail. They are new every morning; great is your faithfulness.

Lamentations 3:22-23 NIV

For the Lord is good. His unfailing love continues forever, and his faithfulness continues to each generation.

Psalm 100:5 NLT

Summing Things Up

In the midst of suffering, God's grace is sufficient. His strength is made perfect in our weaknesses.

Your Own Thoughts

CHAPTER 14

WHEN WE DON'T UNDERSTAND

Can you understand the secrets of God?
His limits are higher than the heavens;
you cannot reach them!
They are deeper than the grave;
you cannot understand them!
His limits are longer than the earth
and wider than the sea.

—

Job 11:7-9 NCV

Sometimes, things happen, and we simply can't understand why. When life takes a turn for the worse, we wonder why, but no matter how hard we think or how desperately we try, we simply cannot understand God's plan. And that's okay with God.

In the Book of Job, God's Word teaches us that He is sovereign, that He reigns over His entire creation (including us), and that He isn't required to answer all our questions.

So, what should we do? Well, for starters, we can recognize God's sovereignty and accept the fact that His secrets are "beyond our reach." Then, we can turn to God's Word for guidance.

The instructions of Proverbs 3:6 are clear: "In all your ways acknowledge Him, and He shall direct your paths." When you think about it, the words in this verse make a powerful promise: If you acknowledge God's sovereignty over every

> There are a lot of things in life that are difficult to understand. Faith allows the soul to go beyond what the eyes can see.
> —John Maxwell

aspect of your life, He will guide your path. So, as you prayerfully consider the path that God intends for you to take, here are things you should do: You should study His Word and be ever-watchful for His signs. You should listen carefully to that inner voice that speaks to you in the quiet moments of your daily devotionals. And, as you continually seek God's unfolding purpose for your life, you should be patient.

Can you trust God even when trusting Him is hard? If you answered yes, congratulations. If you answered no, don't despair, but don't stop praying, either.

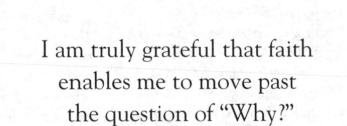

I am truly grateful that faith enables me to move past the question of "Why?"

—

Zig Ziglar

Faith and Trust

Nothing is more disastrous than to study faith, analyze faith, make noble resolves of faith, but never actually to make the leap of faith.

Vance Havner

Faith is to believe what you do not see; the reward of this faith is to see what you believe.

St. Augustine

Faith's wings are clipped by reason's scissors.

R. G. Lee

The popular idea of faith is of a certain obstinate optimism: the hope, tenaciously held in the face of trouble, that the universe is fundamentally friendly and things may get better.

J. I. Packer

Faith is trusting in advance what will only make sense in reverse.

Phillip Yancey

Faith never knows where it is being led, but it loves the One who is leading.

Oswald Chambers

More from God's Word About Faith

For whatever is born of God overcomes the world. And this is the victory that has overcome the world—our faith.

1 John 5:4 NKJV

It is impossible to please God apart from faith. And why? Because anyone who wants to approach God must believe both that he exists and that he cares enough to respond to those who seek him.

Hebrews 11:6 MSG

Let us hold fast the confession of our hope without wavering, for He who promised is faithful.

Hebrews 10:23 NKJV

Trust in the Lord with all your heart, and do not rely on your own understanding; think about Him in all your ways, and He will guide you on the right paths.

Proverbs 3:5-6 HCSB

Those who trust in the Lord are like Mount Zion. It cannot be shaken; it remains forever.

Psalm 125:1 HCSB

Trusting God During Tough Times

Your Heavenly Father may not always reveal Himself as quickly as you would like. And He may not always answer your prayers with a resounding yes. But of this you can be sure: God is sovereign, God is here, God is love, and God intends to use you in wonderful, unexpected ways. He desires to lead you along a path of His choosing, not your choosing. Your challenge is to watch, to listen, to learn . . . and to follow.

Summing Things Up

Sometimes, we simply cannot understand why things happen. But even when we can't understand God's plans, we must trust His plans.

Your Own Thoughts

CHAPTER 15

GIVING ENDURANCE A CHANCE TO GROW

Consider it a great joy, my brothers,
whenever you experience various trials,
knowing that the testing of your faith produces endurance.
But endurance must do its complete work,
so that you may be mature and complete, lacking nothing.

—

James 1:2-4 HCSB

*Dear brothers and sisters, when troubles come your way,
consider it an opportunity for great joy.
For you know that when your faith is tested,
your endurance has a chance to grow. So let it grow,
for when your endurance is fully developed,
you will be perfect and complete, needing nothing.
If you need wisdom, ask our generous God,
and he will give it to you. He will not rebuke you for asking.
But when you ask him, be sure that your faith is in God
alone. Do not waver, for a person with divided loyalty is
as unsettled as a wave of the sea that is blown and tossed by
the wind. Such people should not expect to receive anything
from the Lord. Their loyalty is divided between God
and the world, and they are unstable in everything they do.
So don't be misled, my dear brothers and sisters.
Whatever is good and perfect comes down to us from
God our Father, who created all the lights in the heavens.
He never changes or casts a shifting shadow.
He chose to give birth to us by giving us his true word.
And we, out of all creation, became his prized possession.*

—

James 1:2-8, 16-18 NLT

Who among us wants to endure trials and troubles in order to develop the endurance that's described in the second chapter of James? I don't know about you, but if I could find an easier way to become "perfect and complete," I'd certainly be tempted to take it. Nonetheless, God has plans for me—and for you—plans that are often difficult to understand.

Why, we ask ourselves, must we endure suffering? Why all the pain and heartache? Why, we wonder, doesn't God simply give us all the good and none of the bad?

As a kid, it was easier for me to decipher between good and bad. It was good when I made an A on a test and bad when I made an F. It was good when I cleaned my room and bad when I poured out a whole can of spiders in my mom's tent on our family camping trip. But when I became an adult, I discovered that many things fall into a bittersweet category.

> We had plenty of challenges, some of which were tremendously serious, yet God has enabled us to walk, crawl, limp, or leap—whatever way we could progress—toward wholeness.
> —*Beth Moore*

When we moved away from our hometown to take a job in Atlanta, we were heartbroken to leave our families and the simplicity of small-town South Carolina life. Yet, we were also excited about the new chapter God had for us and the amazing church that had called us to come serve. The whole experience was bittersweet.

Since then, we've gone through some dark valleys, many experiences that contained king-sized quantities of "bitter" and very little "sweet." But we've found comfort in the knowledge that through every trial and every setback, God is molding our spirits. He is the potter; we are the clay. Whatever is good and perfect comes down from Him.

Can you trust God in good times (when it's easy) and hard times (when it's not)? Hopefully so, because you are His prized possession, and His love for you is eternal.

Growth takes place in quietness, in hidden ways, in silence and solitude. The process is not accessible to observation.

Eugene Peterson

Spiritual Growth

God's plan for our guidance is for us to grow gradually in wisdom before we get to the crossroads.

Bill Hybels

God does not discipline us to subdue us, but to condition us for a life of usefulness and blessedness.

Billy Graham

Often God shuts a door in our face so that he can open the door through which he wants us to go.

Catherine Marshall

The trials I experience in the race of life may not seem good to me now, but God promises that they will benefit me later on.

Warren Wiersbe

Transformation will begin in any life—in yours—when you stand up and say: "I'm responsible for the kind of person I am. I am what I've wanted to be. Now I've changed my mind. I'm sorry for what I am and for what I have done. I'm going to be different. God help me."

E. Stanley Jones

More from God's Word About Spiritual Growth

For this reason also, since the day we heard this, we haven't stopped praying for you. We are asking that you may be filled with the knowledge of His will in all wisdom and spiritual understanding.

Colossians 1:9 HCSB

I want their hearts to be encouraged and joined together in love, so that they may have all the riches of assured understanding, and have the knowledge of God's mystery— Christ.

Colossians 2:2 HCSB

But grow in the grace and knowledge of our Lord and Savior Jesus Christ. To Him be the glory both now and to the day of eternity.

2 Peter 3:18 HCSB

Summing Things Up

In good times and hard times, through every trial and every setback, God is molding you. He is the Potter and you are His clay.

Your Own Thoughts

CHAPTER 16

WHAT IF HEALING COMES THROUGH TEARS?

*It will be hard when all these things happen to you.
But after that you will come back to the Lord your God
and obey him, because the Lord your God is
a merciful God. He will not leave you or destroy you.
He will not forget the Agreement with your ancestors,
which he swore to them.*

—

Deuteronomy 4:30-31 NCV

If you've recently experienced a significant loss, you're probably looking for some sort of silver lining around the clouds of hardship. But, if you're like most of us, you may be having trouble finding even a thin thread of silver around those clouds. If so, it's time to remind yourself of these two facts: God's love for you is limitless, and His plans are far greater than your plans.

> Our valleys may be filled with foes and tears, but we can lift our eyes to the hills to see God and the angels.
> —*Billy Graham*

Can healing come through tears? And, can God use your temporary pain for His eternal purposes? The answer to these two questions is yes and yes.

Perhaps you feel like you've been isolated by events and circumstances from which you can never recover. If you have these feelings— and even if these feelings seem very real indeed—you're mistaken. Every difficult circumstance and every painful experience can be used by God for His purposes and for your spiritual growth.

Since God is everywhere, we are free to sense His presence whenever we take the time to quiet our souls and turn our prayers to Him. But sometimes, amid the incessant demands of everyday life, we may turn our thoughts far from God; when we do, we rob ourselves of the peace—God's peace—that is ours for the asking.

Are you exhausted, discouraged, or fearful? Be comforted because God is with you. Are you confused?

Listen to the quiet voice of your Heavenly Father. Are you bitter? Talk with God and seek His guidance. Are you still grieving a loss from long ago? Ask God to heal your heart. He is the Giver of all things good, and He has a plan for spiritual healing and spiritual growth that is designed specifically for you.

Adversity is not simply a tool.
It is God's most effective tool for
the advancement of our spiritual lives.
The circumstances and events that we see as
setbacks are oftentimes the very things that
launch us into periods of intense spiritual
growth. Once we begin to understand this,
and accept it as a spiritual fact of life,
adversity becomes easier to bear.

—

Charles Stanley

About Grief

Those who abandon ship the first time it enters a storm miss the calm beyond. And the rougher the storms weathered together, the deeper and stronger real love grows.

Ruth Bell Graham

Suffering may be someone's fault or it may not be anyone's fault. But if given to God, our suffering becomes an opportunity to experience the power of God at work in our lives and to give glory to Him.

Anne Graham Lotz

When we cry, we allow our bodies to function according to God's design—and we embrace one of the "perks" he offers to relieve our stress.

Barbara Johnson

By ourselves we are not capable of suffering bravely, but the Lord possesses all the strength we lack and will demonstrate His power when we undergo persecution.

Corrie ten Boom

More from God's Word About Hardships and Suffering

For though a righteous man falls seven times, he rises again....
Proverbs 24:16 NIV

The Lord lifts the burdens of those bent beneath their loads. The Lord loves the righteous.

Psalm 146:8 NLT

Come to me, all you who are weary and burdened, and I will give you rest. Take my yoke upon you and learn from me, for I am gentle and humble in heart, and you will find rest for your souls. For my yoke is easy and my burden is light.
Matthew 11:28-30 NIV

Weeping may go on all night, but joy comes with the morning.
Psalm 30:5 NLT

Summing Things Up

God can do anything. He can even bring healing through tears.

Your Own Thoughts

CHAPTER 17

HOW MIGHT GOD PLAN TO USE THIS TRIAL?

Don't fret or worry. Instead of worrying, pray. Let petitions and praises shape your worries into prayers, letting God know your concerns. Before you know it, a sense of God's wholeness, everything coming together for good, will come and settle you down. It's wonderful what happens when Christ displaces worry at the center of your life.

—

Philippians 4:6-7 MSG

Because God sees our lives from an eternal perspective, He has plans that we humans simply cannot understand. But, even when we cannot understand God, we should trust Him.

If you're like most people, you have some sort of plan for your life, an informal list of things you'd like to accomplish before you die. And you can be sure that God has a plan for your life, too, a plan that He understands as thoroughly and completely as He knows you. So, what happens when your plans and God's plans come into conflict? Well, it almost goes without saying, but I'll say it anyway: God always has the last word.

If you're experiencing hardship or pain, and if you can't figure out why, perhaps it's time to put the "why" question aside, at least for now. Perhaps God's plans will be clear to you someday soon, or maybe you won't have all the answers until you finally reach heaven. Either way,

> Suffering is not punishment; it is a work of grace meant to produce eternal fruit. God is preparing us for eternity.
> —Joey Johnson

you can be sure that God is always with you and that He can use your trials for His purposes. So wherever you find yourself—whether on the mountaintops, in the valleys, or at the crossroads of life—rest assured that God has an eternal plan that's perfectly designed for you and your loved ones. Trust His plan today, even if you can't understand it.

Trusting God's Plans

It's incredible to realize that what we do each day has meaning in the big picture of God's plan.

Bill Hybels

God has a plan for the life of every Christian. Every circumstance, every turn of destiny, all things work together for your good and for His glory.

Billy Graham

When the dream of our heart is one that God has planted there, a strange happiness flows into us. At that moment, all of the spiritual resources of the universe are released to help us. Our praying is then at one with the will of God and becomes a channel for the Creator's purposes for us and our world.

Catherine Marshall

God will never lead you where His strength cannot keep you.

Barbara Johnson

God has charged himself with full responsibility for our eternal happiness and stands ready to take over the management of our lives.

A. W. Tozer

What God has started in all of us
He has promised to finish.

—

Gloria Gaither

More from God's Word About God's Plans

"I say this because I know what I am planning for you," says the Lord. "I have good plans for you, not plans to hurt you. I will give you hope and a good future."

Jeremiah 29:11 NCV

People may make plans in their minds, but the Lord decides what they will do.

Proverbs 16:9 NCV

We know that all things work together for the good of those who love God: those who are called according to His purpose.

Romans 8:28 HCSB

The Lord says, "I will guide you along the best pathway for your life. I will advise you and watch over you."

Psalm 32:8 NLT

Summing Things Up

God sees our lives from an eternal perspective, and His plans are beyond our comprehension. So even when we can't understand God, we must trust in the ultimate goodness of His plans.

Your Own Thoughts

CHAPTER 18

WHEN WE CRY OUT IN ANGER

Refrain from anger and turn from wrath;
do not fret—it leads only to evil.

—

Psalm 37:8 NIV

Sometimes, it's very easy to become angry: angry with ourselves, angry with other people, and even angry with God. Sometimes, we face life-threatening situations that shake us to the very core of our souls. But more often than not, our frustrations are of the more mundane variety. More often than not, we are angered not by earth-shaking events, but by the inevitable distractions and disappointments of everyday living: jammed traffic, difficult people, financial headaches, and a near-endless stream of minor inconveniences masquerading as major hardships. Our challenge is this: to display anger when it is appropriate and to rein in our tempers when it is not.

How can we learn to maintain better control over our tempers? We do so by learning to focus our thoughts, not on the inevitable disappointments of life, but instead upon the innumerable blessings that God has given us (Philippians 4:8).

> Anger is the fluid that love bleeds when you cut it.
> —C. S. Lewis

When we allow our faith in God to become the cornerstone and the touchstone of our lives, we cultivate trust in the righteousness of His plans. When we do so, we begin to see God's hand as it works in every aspect of our lives—in good times and in hard times—as He uses every circumstance to fulfill His plan for us.

So the next time you become frustrated by the inevitable challenges of life, do yourself a favor: turn away from anger and turn, instead, to God. Turn to Him, as best you can, with open hands, a clear mind, and a trusting heart. When you do, you'll discover that defeating anger is difficult but not impossible—because with God, all things are possible.

Life is too short to spend it being angry, bored, or dull.

—

Barbara Johnson

The Futility of Anger

What is hatred, after all, other than anger that was allowed to remain, that has become ingrained and deep-rooted? What was anger when it was fresh becomes hatred when it is aged.

St. Augustine

Anger is the noise of the soul; the unseen irritant of the heart; the relentless invader of silence.

Max Lucado

Is there somebody who's always getting your goat? Talk to the Shepherd.

Anonymous

Unrighteous anger feeds the ego and produces the poison of selfishness in the heart.

Warren Wiersbe

Get rid of the poison of built-up anger and the acid of long-term resentment.

Charles Swindoll

More from God's Word About Finding Strength Amid Sadness

O LORD, you are my light; yes, LORD, you light up my darkness.

2 Samuel 22:29 NLT

Though I sit in darkness, the Lord will be my light.

Micah 7:8 HCSB

Unto thee, O my strength, will I sing: for God is my defense, and the God of my mercy.

Psalm 59:17 KJV

Give your burdens to the Lord, and he will take care of you. He will not permit the godly to slip and fall.

Psalm 55:22 NLT

For thou wilt light my candle: the LORD my God will enlighten my darkness.

Psalm 18:28 KJV

Secondhand Anger

Sometimes we are victims of secondhand anger. We may become angry because someone else is angry. Why does this occur? Because anger is a highly contagious emotion. When we spend time with angry people, we, too, tend to become angry. Once again, God's Word offers a solution that doubles as a warning: "Make no friendship with an angry man" (Proverbs 22:24 NKJV). And that's a warning that all of us should take seriously.

Summing Things Up

The next time you become frustrated by the inevitable disappointments of everyday life, do yourself and your loved ones a favor: turn away from anger and turn, instead, to God.

Your Own Thoughts

CHAPTER 19

THE HIDDEN BLESSING OF AFFLICTION

*Blessed be the God and Father of our Lord Jesus Christ,
the Father of mercies and the God of all comfort.
He comforts us in all our affliction, so that we may be able
to comfort those who are in any kind of affliction,
through the comfort we ourselves receive from God.*

—

2 Corinthians 1:3-4 HCSB

All praise to God, the Father of our Lord Jesus Christ.
God is our merciful Father and the source of all comfort.
He comforts us in all our troubles so that we can
comfort others. When they are troubled, we will be able
to give them the same comfort God has given us.
For the more we suffer for Christ, the more God will
shower us with his comfort through Christ.
Even when we are weighed down with troubles,
it is for your comfort and salvation! For when we ourselves
are comforted, we will certainly comfort you.
Then you can patiently endure the same things we suffer.
We are confident that as you share in our sufferings,
you will also share in the comfort God gives us.

—

2 Corinthians 1:3-7 NLT

Who is the first person you call when you are in trouble? Do you call the person who always knows the right thing to say? Or do you call the person who has a broad shoulder to cry on? Or do you call the person who's "been there, done that, and survived"?

We all admire the people who can comfort us, and deep down, all of us want to be the kind of friend others can turn to in their time of need. The bad news, of course, is that the lessons of "good comforting" aren't necessarily learned in online seminary courses or in introductory Bible studies.

In 2 Corinthians 1, we learn that the art of comforting others is a direct result of our own suffering: As God comforts us in our affliction, we learn to comfort others in their affliction. God, through the Holy Spirit, enables us to show His comfort to others.

> No one is beyond His grace. No situation, anywhere on earth, is too hard for God.
> —Jim Cymbala

During Martin's long stay at the Emory medical center, we had a myriad of visitors who came to "comfort" us. Some visitors challenged our spirituality, saying if we really prayed in faith, God would definitely heal Martin. Others informed me that it would be alright if Martin died because I would certainly see him again in heaven one day. Though many of these truths are right and

Biblical, they bruised my heart, and they didn't bring healing.

After long nights of sitting up in the ICU, my favorite words to hear were simpler than deep theological truths. I loved to hear words like "How are you?", "I love you," or, my all-time favorite, the words: "Here's your latte!"

Though I would never wish that kind of season on anyone, I cherish the lessons of comfort I learned in the midst of it. I was comforted by many friends and family, and most of all by God's presence who promised to never leave or forsake that little ICU waiting room. I only pray that I could someday be the type of friend that someone calls on in their darkest day. And rather than bringing easy answers or quick fixes, I hope I remember to bring a few kind words, a simple prayer or two, and, just as importantly, a nice, steamy latte.

What a comfort to know that God is present there in your life, available to meet every situation with you, that you are never left to face any problem alone.

—

Vonette Bright

Finding Comfort and Sharing It

Put your hand into the hand of God. He gives the calmness and serenity of heart and soul.

Mrs. Charles E. Cowman

In Jesus, the service of God and the service of the least of the brethren were one.

Dietrich Bonhoeffer

God's promises are medicine for the broken heart. Let Him comfort you. And, after He has comforted you, try to share that comfort with somebody else. It will do both of you good.

Warren Wiersbe

No matter how crazy or nutty your life has seemed, God can make something strong and good out of it. He can help you grow wide branches for others to use as shelter.

Barbara Johnson

The Scripture says that in the midst of persecution, confusion, wars, and rumors of wars, we are to comfort one another with the knowledge that Jesus Christ is coming back in triumph, glory, and majesty.

Billy Graham

We look at our burdens and
heavy loads, and we shrink from
them. But, if we lift them and
bind them about our hearts,
they become wings,
and on them we can rise
and soar toward God.

—

Mrs. Charles E. Cowman

More from God's Word About Comforting Others

Help each other with your troubles. When you do this, you truly obey the law of Christ.

Galatians 6:2 ICB

As iron sharpens iron, so people can improve each other.

Proverbs 27:17 NCV

A word spoken at the right time is like golden apples on a silver tray.

Proverbs 25:11 HCSB

Let us think about each other and help each other to show love and do good deeds.

Hebrews 10:24 NCV

Summing Things Up

As God comforts us in our affliction, we learn to comfort others in their affliction. God through the Holy Spirit enables us to show to others His comfort.

Your Own Thoughts

CHAPTER 20

HOW CAN WE FIND PEACE AMID SUFFERING?

*When you pass through the waters, I will be with you;
and through the rivers, they shall not overflow you.
When you walk through the fire, you shall not be burned,
nor shall the flame scorch you. For I am the Lord
your God, The Holy One of Israel, your Savior.*

—

Isaiah 43:2-3 NKJV

The comforting words of Isaiah 43 remind us that whenever we experience tough times, God is right there with us. But sometimes, it doesn't seem that way. Sometimes, even though we trust God's promises, we may still experience periods of fear and doubt.

What can we do when life seems to be spinning out of control? Well, we can turn to the world for solutions, but more often than not, we'll be disappointed. Or, we can turn to Jesus for the peace we so desperately desire.

> The fruit of our placing all things in God's hands is the presence of His abiding peace in our hearts.
> —*Hannah Whitall Smith*

The timeless words of John 14:27 remind us that Jesus offers peace, not as the world gives, but as He alone gives: "Peace I leave with you; My peace I give to you; not as the world gives do I give to you. Do not let your heart be troubled, nor let it be fearful" (NASB).

Are you willing to entrust your fears, your hopes, and your life to Jesus? Will you accept the genuine peace that can be yours through Him? Or will you keep rushing after the illusion of "peace and happiness" that the world promises but cannot deliver?

Today, why not claim the genuine peace that is your spiritual birthright? Why not claim the peace of Jesus Christ? It is a peace that depends, not upon your circumstances, but upon your faith. It is a peace unlike any other. It is yours for the asking. So ask. And then share.

God's peace is like a river,
not a pond. In other words,
a sense of health and well-being,
both of which are expressions
of the Hebrew shalom,
can permeate our homes even
when we're in white-water rapids.

—

Beth Moore

Finding Peace

In the center of a hurricane there is absolute quiet and peace. There is no safer place than in the center of the will of God.

Corrie ten Boom

His peace is a direct gift through the personal presence of the Holy Ghost.

Oswald Chambers

The Bible instructs—and experience teaches—that praising God results in our burdens being lifted and our joys being multiplied.

Jim Gallery

That peace, which has been described and which believers enjoy, is a participation of the peace which their glorious Lord and Master himself enjoys.

Jonathan Edwards

To know God as He really is—in His essential nature and character—is to arrive at a citadel of peace that circumstances may storm, but can never capture.

Catherine Marshall

More from God's Word About Peace

The peace of God, which surpasses all understanding, will guard your hearts and minds through Christ Jesus.

Philippians 4:7 NKJV

Be of good comfort, be of one mind, live in peace; and the God of love and peace will be with you.

2 Corinthians 13:11 NKJV

For He is our peace.

Ephesians 2:14 HCSB

God has called us to peace.

1 Corinthians 7:15 NKJV

You, Lord, give true peace to those who depend on you, because they trust you.

Isaiah 26:3 NCV

I have told you these things so that in Me you may have peace. In the world you have suffering. But take courage! I have conquered the world.

John 16:33 HCSB

Find and Sharing His Peace

Are you at peace with the direction of your life? You should be. Even if God's plans for you are uncertain, His love for you is not. And because God keeps His promises, you can be sure that you are loved and protected, now and forever.

Today offers yet another opportunity to welcome the Creator into your heart and share His good news with the world. It's the right thing to do and the peaceful way to live.

Summing Things Up

God offers peace not as the world gives, but as He alone gives. God's peace is far deeper and infinitely richer than anything that the world has to offer. Our challenge is to look only to God for the peace we so desperately desire.

Your Own Thoughts

CHAPTER 21

BEYOND BITTERNESS

*All bitterness, anger and wrath, insult and slander
must be removed from you, along with all wickedness.
And be kind and compassionate to one another,
forgiving one another, just as God
also forgave you in Christ.*

—

Ephesians 4:31-32 HCSB

When hardships happen, it's easy to become bitter: bitter about our circumstances, bitter with family or friends, even bitter about God's refusal to deliver us from the pain. But bitterness is spiritual sickness, a malady to be feared and avoided.

Bitterness will consume your soul; it is dangerous to your emotional health. It can destroy you if you let it . . . so don't let it!

If you are caught up in intense feelings of anger or resentment, you know all too well the destructive power of these emotions. How can you rid yourself of these feelings? First, you must prayerfully ask God to cleanse your heart. Then, you must learn to catch yourself whenever thoughts of bitterness or hatred begin to attack you. Your challenge is this: You must learn to resist negative thoughts before they hijack your emotions.

> Bitterness is its own prison.
> —Max Lucado

Are you mired in the quicksand of bitterness or regret? If so, it's time to free yourself from the mire. So, if there exists even one person—including yourself—against whom you still harbor ill will, it's time to forgive and move on. Bitterness and regret are not part of God's plan for you, but God won't force you to forgive others. It's a job that only you can finish, and the sooner you finish it, the better.

Moving Beyond Bitterness and Blame

Forgiveness is a stunning principle, your ticket out of hate and fear and chaos.

Barbara Johnson

A heart out of tune, out of sync with God's heart, will produce a life of spiritual barrenness and missed opportunities.

Jim Cymbala

When you harbor bitterness, happiness will dock elsewhere.

Anonymous

Bitterness is a spiritual cancer, a rapidly growing malignancy that can consume your life. Bitterness cannot be ignored but must be healed at the very core, and only Christ can heal bitterness.

Beth Moore

Bitterness is the greatest barrier to friendship with God.

Rick Warren

Bitterness is a settled hostility that poisons the whole inner person.

Warren Wiersbe

More from God's Word About Anger and Bitterness

But now you must also put away all the following: anger, wrath, malice, slander, and filthy language from your mouth.

Colossians 3:8 HCSB

But if you harbor bitter envy and selfish ambition in your hearts, do not boast about it or deny the truth. Such "wisdom" does not come down from heaven but is earthly, unspiritual, of the devil. For where you have envy and selfish ambition, there you find disorder and every evil practice.

James 3:14-16 NIV

The Lord says, "Forget what happened before, and do not think about the past. Look at the new thing I am going to do. It is already happening. Don't you see it? I will make a road in the desert and rivers in the dry land."

Isaiah 43:18-19 NCV

Summing Things Up

Bitterness is dangerous to your emotional health. It can destroy you if you let it . . . so don't let it!

Your Own Thoughts

CHAPTER 22

BEYOND WORRY

Jesus said, "Don't let your hearts be troubled.
Trust in God, and trust in me."

—

John 14:1 NCV

I know that I should trust God completely and turn my all troubles over to Him, but sometimes I just can't seem to help myself: sometimes I worry. I worry about big stuff and little stuff; I worry about things I can control, and things I can't; I worry about big problems, medium problems, and even tiny problems. Deep down in my heart, I know that God will provide, but I can't quite seem to get that message through to my head.

I suppose that all of us, even those among us who are the most faithful believers, still worry about things from time to time. Why? Because we are imperfect human beings who possess imperfect faith. Even though we have been given God's assurance of salvation—even though we have received His promise of eternal love and eternal life—we worry.

Jesus understood our concerns when He spoke the reassuring words found in the 6th chapter of Matthew.

Therefore I say to you, do not worry about your life, what you will eat or what you will drink; nor about your body, what you will put on. Is not life more than food and the body more than clothing? Look at the birds of the air, for they neither sow nor reap nor gather into barns; yet your heavenly Father feeds them. Are you not of more value than they? Which of you by worrying can add one cubit to his stature? . . . Therefore do not worry about tomorrow, for tomorrow will worry about its own things. Sufficient for the day is its own trouble. (vv. 25-27, 34 NKJV)

So where is the best place to take our worries? We should take them to God. We should take our troubles to Him, take our fears to Him, take our doubts to Him, take our weaknesses to Him, take our sorrows to Him . . . and leave them all there.

Can you do that today? Can you take your problems to God and trust Him to honor His promises? I hope you can. And I hope I can, too.

Sometimes we want things
we were not meant to have.
Because He loves us,
the Father says no.
Faith is a willingness not to have
what God is not willing to give.

—

Elisabeth Elliot

About Worry

Worry is the senseless process of cluttering up tomorrow's opportunities with leftover problems from today.

Barbara Johnson

God is bigger than your problems. Whatever worries press upon you today, put them in God's hands and leave them there.

Billy Graham

We are not called to be burden-bearers, but cross-bearers and light-bearers. We must cast our burdens on the Lord.

Corrie ten Boom

This life of faith, then, consists in just this—being a child in the Father's house. Let the ways of childish confidence and freedom from care, which so please you and win your heart when you observe your own little ones, teach you what you should be in your attitude toward God.

Hannah Whitall Smith

Worry and anxiety are sand in the machinery of life; faith is the oil.

E. Stanley Jones

Today is the tomorrow
we worried about yesterday.

—

Dennis Swanberg

More from God's Word About Worry

Therefore humble yourselves under the mighty hand of God, that He may exalt you at the proper time, casting all your anxiety on Him, because He cares for you.

1 Peter 5:6-7 NASB

Yea, though I walk through the valley of the shadow of death, I will fear no evil: for thou art with me; thy rod and thy staff they comfort me.

Psalm 23:4 KJV

When my anxious thoughts multiply within me, Your consolations delight my soul.

Psalm 94:19 NASB

Summing Things Up

When you're worried about something, pray about it, and then do your best to turn that problem over to God. Take your troubles to God—and leave them there.

Your Own Thoughts

CHAPTER 23

WORSHIP IN REAL LIFE

*But the hour is coming, and now is, when the true
worshipers will worship the Father in spirit and truth;
for the Father is seeking such to worship Him.
God is Spirit, and those who worship Him
must worship in spirit and truth.*

—

John 4:23-24 NKJV

Worship takes place in church, of course. Those precious hours we spend in the sanctuary are, well . . . precious. But what about the rest of the week? What about those six days when we're more or less on our own, outside the comforting four walls of our houses of worship? That's what I call "worship in real life," and it's vitally important to our spiritual health.

What is worship? I like John Piper's definition. He says that worship is really "worth-ship," our showing His worth. In other words, we can think of worship as our response to who God says He is. But here's the catch: that kind of worship can't take place only on Sunday morning or Wednesday night. It must, by definition, take place all day every day.

Worship in the real world should never be confused with worship in a perfect world. Unless you happen to be Adam or Eve, you don't get to experience worship in a perfect world. You experience worship in a world filled with suffering and sin, sorrow and pain. It's a world where questions abound and answers are often in short supply. And it's precisely because life is tough that we all need worship. We worship in the real life because life is hard and worshiping God is good for our souls.

Will you worship Him today, as best you can, with willing hands, honest prayers, and a loving heart?

It is impossible to worship God
and remain unchanged.

—

Henry Blackaby

About Worship

It's the definition of worship: A hungry heart finding the Father's feast. A searching soul finding the Father's face. A wandering pilgrim spotting the Father's house. Finding God. Finding God seeking us. This is worship. This is a worshiper.

Max Lucado

The fact that we were created to enjoy God and to worship him forever is etched upon our souls.

Jim Cymbala

God asks that we worship Him with our concentrated minds as well as with our wills and emotions. A divided and scattered mind is not effective.

Catherine Marshall

Worship is not taught from the pulpit. It must be learned in the heart.

Jim Elliot

Let us remember therefore this lesson: That to worship our God sincerely we must evermore begin by hearkening to His voice, and by giving ear to what He commands us.

John Calvin

*Happy are those who hear
the joyful call to worship,
for they will walk in the light
of your presence, Lord.*

—

Psalm 89:15 NLT

More from God's Word About Worship

Since we are receiving a Kingdom that cannot be destroyed, let us be thankful and please God by worshiping him with holy fear and awe.

Hebrews 12:28 NLT

But seek first the kingdom of God and His righteousness, and all these things shall be added to you.

Matthew 6:33 NKJV

Worship the Lord your God and . . . serve Him only.

Matthew 4:10 HCSB

For where two or three are gathered together in My name, I am there among them.

Matthew 18:20 HCSB

Summing Things Up

Worship in the real world should never be confused with worship in a perfect world. Here in the real world, we worship God because life is hard and worshiping Him is good for our souls.

Your Own Thoughts

CHAPTER 24

FINDING PEACE AMID THE THORNS

Blessed are you who are hungry now,
because you will be filled.
Blessed are you who weep now,
because you will laugh.

—

Luke 6:21 HCSB

It has taken me a long time to be thankful for the thorn God allowed into our lives. After many sleepless nights, we have finally come to terms with the fact that God has left my husband with certain disabilities. Of course, we have not given up hope of healing; we pray for it daily. But, we are learning that there are even blessings found in the waiting.

Martin's disabilities cause us to limp. We do life a little bit more slowly now. We rely on our church, our family, and our friends. And we are finding that this isn't necessarily a bad thing. Facing a future that sometimes seems bleak, we have to trust God when He says that His plan is good, even though all around us we see calamity.

> Faith looks back and draws courage; hope looks ahead and keeps desire alive.
> —*John Eldredge*

If faith is truly the substance of trusting what we can't see, I believe we are growing in faith. I wish I could tell you why God hasn't removed our thorn, or why He hasn't removed your thorn, but those are answers we may not receive this side of heaven. But I do know that weakness isn't necessarily a bad place to be, especially when you have a strong God on your side.

The best we can hope for in this life is
a knothole peek at the shining
realities ahead. Yet a glimpse is enough.
It's enough to convince our hearts
that whatever sufferings and sorrows
currently assail us aren't worthy
of comparison to that which
waits over the horizon.

—

Joni Eareckson Tada

Faith and Hope

I discovered that sorrow was not to be feared but rather endured with hope and expectancy that God would use it to visit and bless my life.

Jill Briscoe

Hope is nothing more than the expectation of those things which faith has believed to be truly promised by God.

John Calvin

No other religion, no other philosophy promises new bodies, hearts, and minds. Only in the Gospel of Christ do hurting people find such incredible hope.

Joni Eareckson Tada

Oh, remember this: There is never a time when we may not hope in God. Whatever our necessities, however great our difficulties, and though to all appearance help is impossible, yet our business is to hope in God, and it will be found that it is not in vain.

George Mueller

Never yield to gloomy anticipation. Place your hope and confidence in God. He has no record of failure.

Mrs. Charles E. Cowman

More from God's Word About Optimism

The Lord is my light and my salvation; whom shall I fear? The Lord is the strength of my life; of whom shall I be afraid?

Psalm 27:1 KJV

But if we look forward to something we don't have yet, we must wait patiently and confidently.

Romans 8:25 NLT

For God has not given us a spirit of fearfulness, but one of power, love, and sound judgment.

2 Timothy 1:7 HCSB

Be of good courage, and He shall strengthen your heart, all you who hope in the Lord.

Psalm 31:24 NKJV

My cup runs over. Surely goodness and mercy shall follow me all the days of my life; and I will dwell in the house of the Lord forever.

Psalm 23:5-6 NKJV

Three Questions

1. What is your thorn?

2. In what ways has God answered your prayers differently than you expected?

3. How has your thorn taught you to rely on God more, thus strengthening your faith?

Summing Things Up

Amid the thorns of life, we can still find peace: God's peace.

Your Own Thoughts

CHAPTER 25

HE HEARS EACH SPOKEN NEED

❧

The LORD sees every heart and understands
and knows every plan and thought.

—

1 Chronicles 28:9 NLT

Have you ever said a prayer and then wondered, "Is anybody listening?" Well, even if you feel distanced from God, you can be sure that He is never distant from you. And, you can also be sure that He hears every spoken need.

God promises that He is with us wherever we go. He is never absent from our lives or from our world. He is not somewhere "out there"; He is always with us, continuously reshaping our lives and blessing us in ways that we cannot fully understand.

Do you feel discouraged or abandoned? If so, you can be comforted by the thought that God is with you always, listening to your thoughts and prayers, watching your every step. As the demands of life weigh down upon you, you may temporarily lose the sense of God's presence. But, even if you feel distanced from God, He is never distant from you.

> Faith in a prayer-hearing God will make a prayer-loving Christian.
> —Andrew Murray

When you quiet yourself and acknowledge His presence, God will touch your heart and restore your spirits. At this very moment, God is seeking to work in you and through you. Are you willing to let Him?

As we join together in prayer,
we draw on God's enabling might
in a way that multiplies our own
efforts many times over.

—

Shirley Dobson

About Prayer

God delights in the prayers of His children—prayers that express our love for Him, prayers that share our deepest burdens with Him.

Billy Graham

The center of power is not to be found in summit meetings or in peace conferences. It is not in Peking or Washington or the United Nations, but rather where a child of God prays in the power of the Spirit for God's will to be done in her life, in her home, and in the world around her.

Ruth Bell Graham

The Christian on his knees sees more than the philosopher on tiptoe.

D. L. Moody

Obedience is the master key to effective prayer.

Billy Graham

We must leave it to God to answer our prayers in His own wisest way. Sometimes, we are so impatient and think that God does not answer. God always answers! He never fails! Be still. Abide in Him.

Mrs. Charles E. Cowman

More from God's Word About Prayer

The intense prayer of the righteous is very powerful.

James 5:16 HCSB

Rejoice in hope; be patient in affliction; be persistent in prayer.

Romans 12:12 HCSB

Is anyone among you suffering? He should pray. Is anyone cheerful? He should sing praises.

James 5:13 HCSB

Rejoice evermore. Pray without ceasing. In every thing give thanks: for this is the will of God in Christ Jesus concerning you.

1 Thessalonians 5:16-18 KJV

Summing Things Up

God hears each spoken need and responds in His own time, according to a perfect plan that we human beings cannot understand. So even when we don't comprehend God's plans, we can be comforted in the knowledge that He is with us, that He hears us, and that He loves us.

Your Own Thoughts

CHAPTER 26

SHARING HIS JOY

❦

Shout triumphantly to the Lord, all the earth.
Serve the Lord with gladness;
come before Him with joyful songs.

—

Psalm 100:1-2 HCSB

Shout for joy to the LORD, all the earth.
Worship the LORD with gladness;
come before him with joyful songs.
Know that the LORD is God.
It is he who made us, and we are his;
we are his people, the sheep of his pasture.
Enter his gates with thanksgiving
and his courts with praise;
give thanks to him and praise his name.
For the LORD is good and his love
endures forever;
his faithfulness continues through all generations.

Psalm 100 NIV

Psalm 100 reminds us that even when times are tough, we have every reason to celebrate. After all, we are reminded, "the LORD is good; His mercy is everlasting, and His truth endures to all generations."

Yet, sometimes amid the inevitable struggles of life here on earth, we can forfeit—albeit temporarily—the joy that God intends for us.

C. H. Spurgeon, the renowned 19th-century English clergyman, advised, "In the absence of all other joys, the joy of the Lord can fill the soul to the brim." And, he was right: Even when we have no earthly reason to rejoice, we still have a divine reason to celebrate because God has blessed us richly and eternally.

> God gives to us a heavenly gift called joy, radically different in quality from any natural joy.
> —Elisabeth Elliot

In John 15:11, Jesus says, "I have spoken these things to you so that My joy may be in you and your joy may be complete" (HCSB). If your heart is heavy today, open the door of your soul to the Father and to His only begotten Son. Christ offers you His peace and His joy. Accept it and share it freely, just as Christ has freely shared His joy with you.

Genuine Joy

The Christian lifestyle is not one of legalistic do's and don'ts, but one that is positive, attractive, and joyful.

Vonette Bright

Lord, I thank you for the promise of heaven and the unexpected moments when you touch my heartstrings with that longing for my eternal home.

Joni Eareckson Tada

Joy is the direct result of having God's perspective on our daily lives and the effect of loving our Lord enough to obey His commands and trust His promises.

Bill Bright

Where the soul is full of peace and joy, outward surroundings and circumstances are of comparatively little account.

Hannah Whitall Smiith

Our sense of joy, satisfaction, and fulfillment in life increases, no matter what the circumstances, if we are in the center of God's will.

Billy Graham

Joy is the serious business
of heaven.

—

C. S. Lewis

More from God's Word About
Joy and Celebration

This is the day the LORD has made; we will rejoice and be glad in it.

Psalm 118:24 NKJV

Rejoice in the Lord always. I will say it again: Rejoice!

Philippians 4:4 HCSB

A joyful heart is good medicine, but a broken spirit dries up the bones.

Proverbs 17:22 HCSB

And let the peace of the Messiah, to which you were also called in one body, control your hearts. Be thankful.

Colossians 3:15 HCSB

Thanks be to God for His indescribable gift.

2 Corinthians 9:15 HCSB

Let His Joy Become Your Joy

Joy is a way of thinking, a way of behaving, a way of filtering information, and a way of relating to your friends, to your family, and to your Creator. Joy depends, in part, upon your ability to live in the present, not the past—and upon your ability to forgive those who have hurt you.

Christ made it clear to His followers: He intended that His joy would become their joy. And it still holds true today: Christ wants to share His joy with you. Will you let Him?

Summing Things Up

Joy does not depend upon your circumstances, but upon your relationship with God.

Your Own Thoughts

CHAPTER 27

WHY NOT GIVE UP?

For you need endurance,
so that after you have done God's will,
you may receive what was promised.

—

Hebrews 10:36 HCSB

Have you ever been tempted to just give up on life? Have you ever been so tired, or so discouraged, or so worried, or so confused, that you simply wanted to run away and hide from everybody and everything? If so, you're certainly not alone! I believe that the temptation to give up on life is almost universal. All of us endure seasons of hardship that leave us spiritually drained and emotionally spend.

> By perseverance the snail reached the ark.
> —C. H. *Spurgeon*

The next time you find your courage tested to the limit, remember that God is as near as your next breath, and remember that He offers strength and comfort to His children. He is your shield and your strength. Whatever your challenge, whatever your trouble, God can help you persevere. And that's precisely what He'll do if you ask Him.

Perhaps you are in a hurry for God to help you resolve your difficulties. Perhaps you're anxious to earn the rewards that you feel you've already earned from life. Perhaps you're drumming your fingers, impatiently waiting for God to act. If so, be forewarned: God operates on His own timetable, not yours. Sometimes, God may answer your prayers with silence, and when He does, you must patiently wait. In times of trouble, you must remain steadfast and trust in the merciful goodness of your Heavenly Father. Whatever your problem, He can handle it. Your job is to keep persevering until He does.

Determination and faithfulness
are the nails used to build
the house of God's dreams.

Barbara Johnson

Perseverance

Jesus taught that perseverance is the essential element in prayer.

E. M. Bounds

Life will be made or broken at the place where we meet and deal with obstacles.

E. Stanley Jones

In my weakness, I have learned, like Moses, to lean hard on God. The weaker I am, the harder I lean on Him. The harder I lean, the stronger I discover Him to be. The stronger I discover God to be, the more resolute I am in this job He's given me to do.

Joni Eareckson Tada

All rising to a great place is by a winding stair.

Francis Bacon

Keep adding, keep walking, keep advancing; do not stop, do not turn back, do not turn from the straight road.

St. Augustine

God never gives up on you, so don't you ever give up on Him.

Marie T. Freeman

More from God's Word About
Perseverance

Thanks be to God! He gives us the victory through our Lord Jesus Christ. Therefore, my dear brothers, stand firm. Let nothing move you. Always give yourselves fully to the work of the Lord, because you know that your labor in the Lord is not in vain.

1 Corinthians 15:57-58 NIV

I do not consider myself yet to have taken hold of it. But one thing I do: Forgetting what is behind and straining toward what is ahead, I press on toward the goal to win the prize for which God has called me heavenward in Christ Jesus.

Philippians 3:13-14 NIV

Let us not become weary in doing good, for at the proper time we will reap a harvest if we do not give up.

Galatians 6:9 NIV

I have fought a good fight, I have finished my course, I have kept the faith.

2 Timothy 4:7 KJV

But prove yourselves doers of the word, and not merely hearers.

James 1:22 NASB

Strength for the Marathon

The old saying is as true today as it was when it was first spoken: "Life is a marathon, not a sprint." Life, indeed, requires perseverance, so wise travelers select a traveling companion who never tires and never falters. That partner, of course, is God. Are you tired? Ask God for strength. Are you discouraged? Believe in His promises. Are you defeated? Pray as if everything depended upon God, and work as if everything depended upon you.

Summing Things Up

Life is, at times, difficult. When you are tested, call upon God. He can give you the strength to persevere, and that's exactly what you should ask Him to do.

Your Own Thoughts

CHAPTER 28

TURNING YOUR WHY'S INTO HOW'S

*Walking down the street, Jesus saw a man blind from birth.
His disciples asked, "Rabbi, who sinned: this man
or his parents, causing him to be born blind?"
Jesus said, "You're asking the wrong question.
You're looking for someone to blame. There is no such
cause-effect here. Look instead for what God can do."*

—

John 9:1-3 MSG

When Jesus came upon a blind man, His disciples were quick to ask, "Who's to blame?" But, Jesus was quick to correct them. He refused to assign blame. Instead, He asked His disciples to "Look instead for what God can do."

If you're going through tough times, perhaps you, like the disciples, have been asking that age-old question: why? If that's the question you've been asking, don't be surprised if the answer doesn't arrive at your doorstep anytime soon. Occasionally, God answers the "why" question quickly and painlessly, but more often than not, He's in no hurry to explain Himself.

Asking "why" can be helpful for processing grief, which is important. But, my experiences have taught me that focusing too intently on the why's of life is like running on a gerbil wheel: I never seem to get anywhere, and the only product is exhaustion.

> What is God looking for? He is looking for men and women whose hearts are completely His.
> —*Charles Swindoll*

So what's a person to do? I suggest moving beyond the "why" and proceeding directly to the "how" by asking yourself, "How might God use my trial to glorify Himself."

If you're enduring hardship, and if you've been suffering for a while, perhaps it's now time to stop asking why and instead ask yourself how you can bring glory to your Heavenly Father. I have no doubt that God can use your tough times for His glory. Will you let Him?

Righteousness and Praise

Impurity is not just a wrong action; impurity is the state of mind and heart and soul which is just the opposite of purity and wholeness.

A. W. Tozer

Christianity says we were created by a righteous God to flourish and be exhilarated in a righteous environment. God has "wired" us in such a way that the more righteous we are, the more we'll actually enjoy life.

Bill Hybels

When we do what is right, we have contentment, peace, and happiness.

Beverly LaHaye

Have your heart right with Christ, and he will visit you often, and so turn weekdays into Sundays, meals into sacraments, homes into temples, and earth into heaven.

C. H. Spurgeon

The great thing is to be found at one's post as a child of God, living each day as though it were our last, but planning as though our world might last a hundred years.

C. S. Lewis

A life growing in its purity
and devotion will be
a more prayerful life.

—

E. M. Bounds

More from God's Word About Praise

Praise him, all you people of the earth, for he loves us with unfailing love; the faithfulness of the Lord endures forever. Praise the Lord!

Psalm 117 NLT

I will praise the Lord at all times, I will constantly speak his praises.

Psalm 34:1 NLT

Through Him then, let us continually offer up a sacrifice of praise to God, that is, the fruit of lips that give thanks to His name.

Hebrews 13:15 NASB

Is anyone happy? Let him sing songs of praise.

James 5:13 NIV

Summing Things Up

If you're enduring hardship, perhaps it's time to move beyond the "why" and proceed directly to the "how" by asking yourself, "How might God use my trial to glorify Himself?"

Your Own Thoughts

CHAPTER 29

SONG WRITING ACCORDING TO PSALM 40

Many, LORD my God, are the wonders you have done,
the things you planned for us. None can compare with you;
were I to speak and tell of your deeds,
they would be too many to declare.

—

Psalm 40:5 NIV

Ever thought about writing a worship song? It's quite a weighty endeavor, especially considering that our entire reason for existence on this earth is to lift up the praises of our Creator! But, rather than tuning in to the latest fad and formula, why not look to the most famous worship songwriter in history?

Psalm 40 is one of King David's best-known songs, having been adapted to music by artists from Stravinsky to Bono. What aspects of this text make it so powerful? I believe that the first three verses alone speak volumes about David's motivation in singing to His God:

1. I waited patiently for the LORD; he turned to me and heard my cry.

2. He lifted me out of the slimy pit, out of the mud and mire; he set my feet on a rock and gave me a firm place to stand.

3. He put a new song in my mouth, a hymn of praise to our God.

Though it is not my desire to minimize this scripture to merely a blueprint for all worship songs, I do believe it is important that we recognize some key components of this song that give it such impact.

First, David begins with the incorporation of his story. David's testimony, like many of ours, was filled with its share of highlights and lowlights. As a man after God's own heart, he had faith enough to defeat giants and rule nations. Yet, he fell into the most grievous sins, committing adultery and then covering it up with murder. Though the pit of David's sin was deep, he was never out of reach of God's mighty hand of redemption. Where David failed, God restored. Where David waited on the Lord, God showed up in His perfect timing, bringing the utmost glory to Himself! David's personal experience is the basis of his song.

Secondly, we see David's response: the declaration of God's glory. David sings a new song to God, a song of praise and thanksgiving. And why a new song? Could it be because God's mercies are new every morning? Could it be that in every twist and turn of David's journey he discovered new and fresh reasons to sing God's praises?

Lastly, we see David's expectation of the extraordinary. David proclaims God's goodness for this distinct purpose: that many will hear and put their trust in the Lord. David believes that God will do extraordinary things through his new song, not because of the greatness of his songs, but because of the greatness of his God. And, if the sole purpose of our existence is to give praises to our Creator, doesn't it make sense that God would delight in putting these new songs in our hearts?

> Our faith grows by expression. If we want to keep our faith, we must share it. We must act.
> —*Billy Graham*

So what's your story? What pit has God pulled you out of? From what miry clay is God currently redeeming you? And do you believe that your personal testimony could be used to bring many to salvation? God's Word tells us that the church is advancing and the gates of hell will not prevail. As composers of our own stories and our own songs, we have the opportunity to become part of the greatest mission ever. Will we boldly sing our new songs? Will we sing them while there's still time?

There is a glorified Man on the right hand
of the Majesty in heaven
faithfully representing us there.
We are left for a season among men;
let us faithfully represent Him here.

—

A. W. Tozer

Sharing Our Stories

Your light is the truth of the Gospel message itself as well as your witness as to Who Jesus is and what He has done for you. Don't hide it.

Anne Graham Lotz

Every believer may be brought to understand that the only object of his life is to help to make Christ King on the earth.

Andrew Murray

My personal experience is often more acceptable to an unbeliever or skeptic than any historical facts and evidences that I could rattle off.

Becky Tirabassi

The sermon of your life in tough times ministers to people more powerfully than the most eloquent speaker.

Bill Bright

Usually it is those who know Him that bring Him to others. That is why the Church, the whole body of Christians showing Him to one another, is so important.

C. S. Lewis

More from God's Word About
Sharing the Good News

For God has not given us a spirit of fear and timidity, but of power, love, and self-discipline. So you must never be ashamed to tell others about our Lord.

2 Timothy 1:7-8 NLT

But respect Christ as the holy Lord in your hearts. Always be ready to answer everyone who asks you to explain about the hope you have.

1 Peter 3:15 NCV

And I say to you, anyone who acknowledges Me before men, the Son of Man will also acknowledge him before the angels of God; but whoever denies Me before men will be denied before the angels of God.

Luke 12:8-9 HCSB

You are the light of the world. A city that is set on a hill cannot be hidden. Nor do they light a lamp and put it under a basket, but on a lampstand, and it gives light to all who are in the house. Let your light so shine before men, that they may see your good works and glorify your Father in heaven.

Matthew 5:14–16 NKJV

*Whatever I tell you in the dark,
speak in the light;
and what you hear in the ear,
preach on the housetops.*

—

Matthew 10:27 NKJV

Summing Things Up

You have an important story to tell: yours. And you have a new song to sing—a song that can become an integral part of the greatest mission ever: God's mission. Will you boldly sing your song while there's still time?

Your Own Thoughts

CHAPTER 30

THE BLESSING OF THE BIBLE

Heaven and earth will pass away,
but My words will never pass away.

—

Matthew 24:35 HCSB

I have chosen to end these devotionals by reminding you of the promises of scripture and of the blessings we find in the Bible.

The victory has been won and heaven awaits us, but the journey still seems so long. I yearn for the day of His returning, but how do I live in the midst of the carpool lines and bounced checks? What can sustain my soul as I wait upon the Lord?

I have found His Word to truly be a lamp to my feet and a light to my path. Though I cannot see the landscape of the future, God's Word gives me a sure foundation for each next step and His Spirit gives me the hope to actually take that step. We are so blessed to have God's very words to cling to, and His sweet whispers to our soul, reminding us that He is with us and the He will never forsake us.

> Help me, Lord, to be a student of Your Word, that I might be a better servant in Your world.
> —*Jim Gallery*

God's Word can be used as a banner over you, giving you strength for hard days and a security blanket to sleep with at night. God's promises are a balm for every wounded soul and the defense for every trampled saint. So, whatever your need is, be blessed today by the promises of God. Memorize them. Write them on sticky notes for your dashboard or index cards for your wallet. Cling to His Word like the next breath you breathe.

Weave the unveiling fabric
of God's word through
your heart and mind.
It will hold strong,
even if the rest of life unravels.

—

Gigi Graham Tchividjian

God's Word

Prayer and the Word are inseparably linked together. Power in the use of either depends on the presence of the other.

Andrew Murray

I need the spiritual revival that comes from spending quiet time alone with Jesus in prayer and in thoughtful meditation on His Word.

Anne Graham Lotz

Either God's Word keeps you from sin, or sin keeps you from God's Word.

Corrie ten Boom

God has given us all sorts of counsel and direction in his written Word; thank God, we have it written down in black and white.

John Eldredge

Words fail to express my love for this Holy Book, my gratitude for its author, for His love and goodness. How shall I thank him for it?

Lottie Moon

More from God's Word About the Blessing of Scripture

But the word of the Lord endures forever. And this is the word that was preached as the gospel to you.

1 Peter 1:25 HCSB

All Scripture is inspired by God and is profitable for teaching, for rebuking, for correcting, for training in righteousness, so that the man of God may be complete, equipped for every good work.

2 Timothy 3:16-17 HCSB

For the word of God is living and effective and sharper than any two-edged sword, penetrating as far as to divide soul, spirit, joints, and marrow; it is a judge of the ideas and thoughts of the heart.

Hebrews 4:12 HCSB

The one who is from God listens to God's words. This is why you don't listen, because you are not from God.

John 8:47 HCSB

For I am not ashamed of the gospel, because it is God's power for salvation to everyone who believes.

Romans 1:16 HCSB

Nobody ever outgrows Scripture;
the book widens and deepens
with our years.

—

C. H. Spurgeon

Summing Things Up

God's promises can give you comfort, and His wisdom can give you direction. Cling to God's Word today, tomorrow, and forever.

Your Own Thoughts

Blessed is a man who endures trials,
because when he passes the test
he will receive the crown of life
that He has promised
to those who love Him.

—

James 1:12 HCSB

BIBLE VERSES TO CONSIDER

FEAR

For God has not given us a spirit of fear, but of power and of love and of a sound mind.

2 Timothy 1:7 NLT

Do not fear, for I am with you; do not be afraid, for I am your God. I will strengthen you; I will help you; I will hold on to you with My righteous right hand.

Isaiah 41:10 HCSB

I leave you peace; my peace I give you. I do not give it to you as the world does. So don't let your hearts be troubled or afraid.

John 14:27 NCV

And Jesus answered, "Why are you afraid? You have so little faith!" Then he stood up and rebuked the wind and waves, and suddenly all was calm.

Matthew 8:26 NLT

Even though I walk through the valley of the shadow of death, I will fear no evil, for you are with me; your rod and your staff, they comfort me.

Psalm 23:4 NIV

WORRY

Give all your worries and cares to God, for he cares about what happens to you.

1 Peter 5:6 NLT

The Lord himself will go before you. He will be with you; he will not leave you or forget you. Don't be afraid and don't worry.

Deuteronomy 31:8 NCV

I will be with you when you pass through the waters . . . when you walk through the fire . . . the flame will not burn you. For I the Lord your God, the Holy One of Israel, and your Savior.

Isaiah 43:2-3 HCSB

Therefore do not worry about tomorrow, for tomorrow will worry about itself. Each day has enough trouble of its own.

Matthew 6:34 NIV

Give your worries to the Lord, and he will take care of you. He will never let good people down.

Psalm 55:22 NCV

PRAYER

"Relax, Daniel," he continued, "don't be afraid. From the moment you decided to humble yourself to receive understanding, your prayer was heard, and I set out to come to you."

Daniel 10:12 MSG

If you don't know what you're doing, pray to the Father. He loves to help. You'll get his help, and won't be condescended to when you ask for it. Ask boldly, believingly, without a second thought. People who "worry their prayers" are like wind-whipped waves. Don't think you're going to get anything from the Master that way, adrift at sea, keeping all your options open.

James 1:5-8 MSG

Rejoice always, pray without ceasing, in everything give thanks; for this is the will of God in Christ Jesus for you.

1 Thessalonians 5:16-18 NKJV

I want men everywhere to lift up holy hands in prayer, without anger or disputing.

1 Timothy 2:8 NIV

WORSHIP

A time is coming and has now come when the true worshipers will worship the Father in spirit and truth, for they are the kind of worshipers the Father seeks. God is spirit, and his worshipers must worship in spirit and in truth.

John 4:23-24 NIV

If any man thirst, let him come unto me, and drink.

John 7:37 KJV

For it is written, "You shall worship the Lord your God, and Him only you shall serve."

Matthew 4:10 NKJV

But seek first his kingdom and his righteousness, and all these things will be given to you as well.

Matthew 6:33 NIV

God lifted him high and honored him far beyond anyone or anything, ever, so that all created beings in heaven and earth, even those long ago dead and buried, will bow in worship before this Jesus Christ, and call out in praise that he is the Master of all.

Philippians 2:9-11 MSG

MIRACLES

Is anything impossible for the Lord?

Genesis 18:14 HCSB

I assure you: The one who believes in Me will also do the works that I do. And he will do even greater works than these, because I am going to the Father.

John 14:12 HCSB

Looking at them, Jesus said, "With men it is impossible, but not with God, because all things are possible with God."

Mark 10:27 HCSB

You are the God who works wonders; You revealed Your strength among the peoples.

Psalm 77:14 HCSB

God verified the message by signs and wonders and various miracles and by giving gifts of the Holy Spirit whenever he chose to do so.

Hebrews 2:4 NLT

GOD'S PLAN

And we know that in all things God works for the good of those who love him, who have been called according to his purpose.

Romans 8:28 NIV

The Lord shatters the plans of nations and thwarts all their schemes. But the Lord's plans stand firm forever; his intentions can never be shaken.

Psalm 33:10-11 NLT

Trust the Lord your God with all your heart and lean not on your own understanding; in all your ways acknowledge him, and he will make your paths straight.

Proverbs 3:5-6 NIV

There is one thing I always do. Forgetting the past and straining toward what is ahead, I keep trying to reach the goal and get the prize for which God called me . . . .

Philippians 3:13-14 NCV

GOD'S LOVE

We know how much God loves us, and we have put our trust in him. God is love, and all who live in love live in God, and God lives in them.

1 John 4:16 NLT

As the Father loved Me, I also have loved you; abide in My love.

John 15:9 NKJV

For God so loved the world, that he gave his only begotten Son, that whosoever believeth in him should not perish, but have everlasting life.

John 3:16 KJV

The unfailing love of the Lord never ends! By his mercies we have been kept from complete destruction.

Lamentations 3:22 NLT

His banner over me was love.

Song of Solomon 2:4 KJV

ENCOURAGEMENT

So encourage each other and give each other strength, just as you are doing now.

1 Thessalonians 5:11 NCV

He comes alongside us when we go through hard times, and before you know it, he brings us alongside someone else who is going through hard times so that we can be there for that person just as God was there for us.

2 Corinthians 1:4 MSG

Encourage each other. Live in harmony and peace. Then the God of love and peace will be with you.

2 Corinthians 13:11 NLT

So don't lose a minute in building on what you've been given, complementing your basic faith with good character, spiritual understanding, alert discipline, passionate patience, reverent wonder, warm friendliness, and generous love, each dimension fitting into and developing the others.

2 Peter 1:5-7 MSG

Watch the way you talk. Let nothing foul or dirty come out of your mouth. Say only what helps, each word a gift.

Ephesians 4:29 MSG

ATTITUDE

A miserable heart means a miserable life; a cheerful heart fills the day with a song.

Proverbs 15:15 MSG

For the word of God is living and active. Sharper than any double-edged sword, it penetrates even to dividing soul and spirit, joints and marrow; it judges the thoughts and attitudes of the heart.

Hebrews 4:12 NIV

Therefore, since Christ suffered in his body, arm yourselves also with the same attitude, because he who has suffered in his body is done with sin. As a result, he does not live the rest of his earthly life for evil human desires, but rather for the will of God.

1 Peter 4:1-2 NIV

Your attitude should be the same as that of Christ Jesus: Who, being in very nature God, did not consider equality with God something to be grasped, but made himself nothing, taking the very nature of a servant, being made in human likeness. And being found in appearance as a man, he humbled himself and became obedient to death—even death on a cross!

Philippians 2:5-8 NIV

DIFFICULT DAYS

We take the good days from God—why not also the bad days?

Job 2:10 MSG

We are hard pressed on every side, yet not crushed; we are perplexed, but not in despair.

2 Corinthians 4:8 NKJV

Now I take limitations in stride, and with good cheer, these limitations that cut me down to size—abuse, accidents, opposition, bad breaks. I just let Christ take over! And so the weaker I get, the stronger I become.

2 Corinthians 12:10 MSG

Consider it pure joy, my brothers, whenever you face trials of many kinds, because you know that the testing of your faith develops perseverance.

James 1:2-3 NIV

Whatever has been born of God conquers the world. This is the victory that has conquered the world: our faith.

1 John 5:4 HCSB

ANGER

And the servant of the Lord must not strive; but be gentle unto all men, apt to teach, patient; in meekness instructing those that oppose themselves . . . .

2 Timothy 2:24-25 KJV

Let all bitterness, and wrath, and anger, and clamor, and evil speaking, be put away from you, with all malice: and be ye kind one to another, tender-hearted, forgiving one another, even as God for Christ's sake hath forgiven you.

Ephesians 4:31-32 KJV

But I tell you that men will have to give account on the day of judgment for every careless word they have spoken. For by your words you will be acquitted, and by your words you will be condemned.

Matthew 12:36-37 NIV

But I tell you that anyone who is angry with his brother is subject to judgment.

Matthew 5:22 NIV

A patient man has great understanding, but a quick-tempered man displays folly.

Proverbs 14:29 NIV

INTEGRITY

Till I die, I will not deny my integrity. I will maintain my righteousness and never let go of it; my conscience will not reproach me as long as I live.

Job 27:5-6 NIV

People with integrity have firm footing, but those who follow crooked paths will slip and fall.

Proverbs 10:9 NLT

The integrity of the upright will guide them.

Proverbs 11:3 NKJV

Love and truth form a good leader; sound leadership is founded on loving integrity.

Proverbs 20:28 MSG

Not only so, but we also rejoice in our sufferings, because we know that suffering produces perseverance; perseverance, character; and character, hope.

Romans 5:3-4 NIV

ACCEPTANCE

Shall I not drink from the cup the Father has given me?
John 18:11 NLT

He is the Lord. Let him do what he thinks is best.
1 Samuel 3:18 NCV

The Lord says, "Forget what happened before, and do not think about the past. Look at the new thing I am going to do. It is already happening. Don't you see it? I will make a road in the desert and rivers in the dry land."
Isaiah 43:18-19 NCV

He said, "I came naked from my mother's womb, and I will be stripped of everything when I die. The Lord gave me everything I had, and the Lord has taken it away. Praise the name of the Lord!"
Job 1:21 NLT

Give in to God, come to terms with him and everything will turn out just fine.
Job 22:21 MSG

GRATITUDE

Everything created by God is good, and nothing is to be rejected, if it is received with gratitude; for it is sanctified by means of the word of God and prayer.

1 Timothy 4:4-5 NASB

As you therefore have received Christ Jesus the Lord, so walk in Him, having been firmly rooted and now being built up in Him and established in your faith, just as you were instructed, and overflowing with gratitude.

Colossians 2:6-7 NASB

Let the message about the Messiah dwell richly among you, teaching and admonishing one another in all wisdom, and singing psalms, hymns, and spiritual songs, with gratitude in your hearts to God.

Colossians 3:16 HCSB

Therefore, since we receive a kingdom which cannot be shaken, let us show gratitude, by which we may offer to God an acceptable service with reverence and awe . . . .

Hebrews 12:28 NASB

OPTIMISM

But if we look forward to something we don't have yet, we must wait patiently and confidently.

Romans 8:25 NLT

Make me hear joy and gladness.

Psalm 51:8 NKJV

My cup runs over. Surely goodness and mercy shall follow me all the days of my life; and I will dwell in the house of the Lord Forever.

Psalm 23:5-6 NKJV

I can do everything through him that gives me strength.

Philippians 4:13 NIV

For God has not given us a spirit of fear, but of power and of love and of a sound mind.

2 Timothy 1:7 NLT

HOPE

The lines of purpose in your lives never grow slack, tightly tied as they are to your future in heaven, kept taut by hope.

Colossians 1:5 MSG

Let us hold fast the confession of our hope without wavering, for He who promised is faithful.

Hebrews 10:23 NASB

Now faith is the substance of things hoped for, the evidence of things not seen.

Hebrews 11:1 KJV

This hope we have as an anchor of the soul, a hope both sure and steadfast.

Hebrews 6:19 NASB

Full of hope, you'll relax, confident again; you'll look around, sit back, and take it easy.

Job 11:18 MSG

LAURA STORY is a songwriter, a worship leader, an artist and yet is an unassuming woman. Her Grammy nominated songs including "Blessings" and Chris Tomlin's "Indescribable" have brought hope to millions around the world. But she would never tell you that. Traveling for concerts, leading worship at Perimeter Church and loving life with her husband Martin in Atlanta, Georgia are everyday gifts of mercy in her life she shares.

For more information visit:

www.laurastorymusic.com   www.facebook.com/laurastory

www.twitter.com/LauraStoryMusic